7623 38

P9-CSG-344

THE SWEDISH WAY
TO PARENT AND PLAY

Kristina Henkel and Marie Tomičić

Tranlsated by Paulina Essunger

THE SWEDISH WAY
TO PARENT AND PLAY

Advice for Raising Gender-Equal Kids

THE COUNTRYMAN PRESS
A division of W. W. Norton & Company
Independent Publishers Since 1923

Copyright © 2009 by Kristina Henkel and Marie Tomičić
Design: Mia Lidbom www.spektrum.nu
Illustrations © by Emili Svensson www.emilisvensson.com
Translation copyright © 2020 by Paulina Essunger

For information about permission to reproduce selections from this book, write to
Permissions, The Countryman Press, 500 Fifth Avenue, New York, NY 10110

For information about special discounts for bulk purchases, please contact
W. W. Norton Special Sales at specialsales@wwnorton.com or 800-233-4830

Manufacturing by Versa Press
Production manager: Devon Zahn

Library of Congress Cataloging-in-Publication Data

Names: Henkel, Kristina, 1981– author. | Tomičić, Marie, 1969– author.
Title: The Swedish way to parent and play : advice for raising gender-equal kids / Kristina Henkel and Marie
    Tomičić; translated by Paulina Essunger.
Other titles: Ge ditt barn 100 möjligheter istället för 2. English
Identifiers: LCCN 2019033461 | ISBN 9781682684306 (paperback) | ISBN 9781682684313 (epub)
Subjects: LCSH: Sex role in children. | Equality. | Play. | Parenting.
Classification: LCC BF723.S42 H4613 2019 | DDC 155.4/182—dc23
LC record available at https://lccn.loc.gov/2019033461

The Countryman Press
www.countrymanpress.com

A division of W. W. Norton & Company, Inc.
500 Fifth Avenue, New York, NY 10110
www.wwnorton.com

978-1-68268-430-6 (pbk.)

10 9 8 7 6 5 4 3 2 1

"All human beings are born free and equal in dignity and rights."

—ARTICLE 1 OF THE UN UNIVERSAL DECLARATION OF HUMAN RIGHTS

"All children are of equal value. You are unique. You and all other children and youth are to be respected. It does not matter what kind of family you have, what country you are from, what language you speak, what you believe in, what gender you are, with whom you fall in love, or whether you have a disability."

—THE SWEDISH PUBLIC ADVOCATE FOR CHILDREN

Welcome

It's been a decade since we wrote the first lines of this book in Swedish. Nevertheless, the content is still current. That's because gender equality is about freedom and rights and power: the power to impact our own lives and our society. Equality doesn't happen on its own or automatically increase over time. It takes courageous and stubborn people who have the strength to change and to advocate.

We would love to be able to cross off a number of gender traps and say, "That's all in the past now." But we are not there, yet. This edition includes all the old gender traps. And we've even added some new ones. Some of these are about boys and violence, because violence is a major societal problem. We've also written more about gender identity, because binary norms are beginning to soften. The gender-neutral pronoun *hen* is used by Swedish media and on blogs and TV shows; the singular *they* is becoming more common in English. More and more children are also challenging gender categories and creating their own identities.

Over the years, we've heard wonderful things about our book, how it's helped people see everyday gender inequalities and has increased gender equality for children. We want to extend our heartfelt thanks for all these wonderful comments! If you're reading the book for the first time, we hope you will be inspired to think about and work on gender equality in new ways. If we work together, maybe we can cross off a few gender traps in time for the next edition. The children will be better off for it!

Kristina Henkel and Marie Tomičić

Contents

"My child was treated totally differently depending on whether she wore a red hat with flowers or a green hat with stripes with her dark blue overalls. When she wore the red one with the flowers, she'd be told that she looked very pretty. When she wore the green one, she'd be told that she looked very lively and strong."

—KRISTINA HENKEL

"Adults told my son that his white sneakers with sparkles were girls' shoes. He was seven and really proud of having chosen those shoes himself."

—MARIE TOMIČIĆ

Pep Talk

Imagine if Hugo and Omar could hug each other without being teased. Imagine if Omar were allowed to cry just like Adriana. Imagine if Ella didn't have to clean up when Gustav made a mess. Imagine if Gustav could play with dolls. Imagine if all children were allowed to be how they want to be. Imagine if we, as adults, could stop limiting our children.

This book is about how and when our children are gendered and made into girls or boys. It's about gender traps and cruxes. We call them "traps" because they're easy to fall into and they limit our children; "cruxes" because the questions are complex, and simple solutions cannot always be found. Gender traps and cruxes result in children being treated one-dimensionally. This, in turn, limits their potential to develop into free and unique individuals.

The gendering of children really jumped out at us once we had our own kids. Even though we'd often been assigned stereotypical roles as girls or women—roles we didn't always feel comfortable in—we didn't expect our children to be gendered so

To gender (verb) = To sort children, adults, toys, etc. as feminine or masculine, assign them different properties and values, and place different expectations on them.

Gender (noun) = Socially constructed sex. Ideas about what is considered feminine and masculine. These ideas can change over time.

13

frequently and to such an extent. We also realized that, often, it wasn't done on purpose; it happened at a subconscious level.

Oh, you are such good girls!

The gendering starts before a child is even born, during pregnancy. Most people are very curious (*Do you know if you're having a boy or a girl?*) and look for clues. Everything, from the shape of the belly, to the heart rate, to how much the baby is kicking, is interpreted as some kind of sign. Once born, boys and girls are dressed in different kinds of clothes and in different colors. We speak to them using different tones of voice, using different words; when they cry, we interpret their cries differently. We attribute different characteristics to girls and boys, and we encourage them to behave differently. All in all, throughout their first years of life, children undergo a number of rituals that mold them into girls or boys. All of this occurs as if it were totally self-evident that it should be this way. Since childhood, we have been told that there are and should be differences between boys and girls; however, we don't always consider the consequences for

Do we have any strong boys around here?

the children. We don't consider that when we gender children, we approach them one-dimensionally. We don't take into account the inequalities we create.

In this book, we want to show easy ways of giving children more options, by treating them as individuals instead of as either girls or boys. The truth is, in spite of all the talk about gender equality and despite most people agreeing that equality is important and valuable, it's not always that easy to take the step from thought to action. How, then, do we actually create gender equality?

We have grouped the gender traps and cruxes into six chapters, each of which illustrates a different aspect of gender inequality. The examples are taken from everyday life, since that's where we're formed as individuals, children and adults alike: at the dinner table, during story time, while playing. These are the moments—though they may seem small and insignificant—when we create reality and can foster gender equality. When considered in isolation, any gender trap may seem benign, but, taken together, they indicate a structure in our society that gives the children we sort into the "girl" category one set of opportunities and those we sort into the "boy" category, another.

No, hair ties are just for girls.

Gender equality (noun) = Giving all human beings—adults as well as children—equal opportunities, rights, and responsibilities, irrespective of gender.

15

We also offer suggestions for how to think and act in new ways in order to open up opportunities for children in the midst of everyday gender stereotyping. These suggestions are meant to inspire; as a reader, you will have your own ideas. Some suggestions will be easier to put into practice than others. Learning to do things differently may take a while, and it will probably take even longer before it comes naturally. But don't give up! Little things make great things possible.

Because preschool is such an important part of the lives of small children, we have chosen to dedicate a separate chapter to it, in which we offer suggestions to preschool teachers and parents about how to raise the issue of gender equality. The book concludes with an explanatory model of how gender inequality arises.

This book is aimed at parents and other adults who come into contact with young children, and it builds on everyday experiences. The quotes and speech bubbles are drawn from what we've experienced in our professional and personal lives. They're also based on a survey of parents and on interviews with companies and municipalities. For privacy, all the names in the book have been changed. In some cases, the quotes have been altered, but the spirit of the remarks is the same.

Some will say that we, ourselves, fall into gender traps, since we generalize and categorize in terms of girls and boys. And this is true. We're aware that real life is complex, and that there is more variation in terms of how girls and boys are treated than depicted in this book. The point of generalizing is to show the existing patterns that our children face. Without generalizations, it's difficult to see what needs to change so that children can be offered more ways of being.

Gender equality is important for all children. The point is not (at all) that all boys should wear dresses or that girls cannot play with dolls. It's not about making everyone the same or about taking anything away. Gender equality is about variety; it's about showing all children 100 ways of being instead of two.

With hope for change,
Kristina Henkel and Marie Tomičić

19

Beyond Hitting vs. Hugging

More Ways of Playing

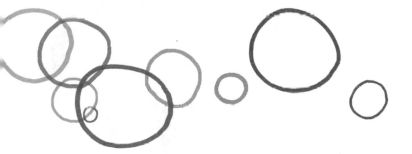

22

Barbie and Batman

Two dolls. Both have names that start with the letter *B*. Apart from that, they couldn't be more different. Barbie is a classic toy for girls, while Batman is aimed at boys. If we take a closer look at Barbie, we see that she needs shoes in order to stand, since her feet are made to fit in high-heeled shoes. (And even with them, she can't really stand on her own!) It's rare for her legs to be bendable, and it's hard for Barbie to grip anything other than her small purse. Barbie is slender, with large eyes and large breasts: a fashion doll to dress and undress. Batman's body is firm and muscular, and he can stand on his own. His hands are made to grab hold of different objects, and, in contrast to Barbie, his eyes are small or even completely hidden behind a mask. Batman's jaw is set in a firm expression, unsmiling, like the contemporary ideal for men.

When a child plays with the Batman doll, the doll is typically turned away, not facing the child. Playing with Batman is seldom a question of dressing and undressing, but more about the doll gliding through the air, jumping, flying a helicopter, running, or using different weapons to attack the enemy. Playing like this teaches independence, courage, and feeling unafraid. Batman does not signal that he needs to be taken care of, and the toy does not encourage hugs or intimacy.

Playing with Barbie often is about changing her clothes and making her look nice, so the doll is often turned toward the child. Playing like this, children focus on communication, interaction, and relationships. That the ways of playing differ so much is also due to human characteristics and skills being attributed to Barbie. It's not as easy to let Barbie become invisible or have her search for underground passages, as it is with Batman, since Batman already has an air of the supernatural, thanks to his fantastic cape and his fast Batmobile. Batman rarely gets to care for the horses or rearrange the furniture in the dollhouse.

Batman, Spider-Man, and the Teenage Mutant Ninja Turtles are seldom referred to as dolls. They are figures. To be on the safe side, the manufacturer adds the label "action"— *action figures*—lest anyone not understand that these toys are all about fast-paced exciting events and adventure. The crux with fashion dolls and action figures is that they send girls and boys the message that they are supposed to be different—that girls are supposed to devote themselves to clothes and looks, while boys are supposed to save the world and fight evil. Girls and boys are, in other words, encouraged to adopt and practice very different roles.

I'm a Daddy-Batman

In 1974, Sweden introduced parental leave benefits that give both mothers and fathers the right to stay home from work with pay in order to take care of their children.
—Statistics Sweden

In 2015 in the US, about 90% of women and 7% of men used parental leave, much of it unpaid.
—Jay L. Zagorsky, "Divergent Trends in US Maternity and Paternity Leave, 1994–2015," *American Journal of Public Health*, 2017

Suggestions

Create things with children. Let them sew capes and purses for both Batman and Barbie. Start by making a drawing and a pattern for the projects.

Assign new roles to Barbie, Batman, and similar dolls. Batman can pick up the Batchildren from day care and then quietly drive home. With kids in the car, the Batmobile can't be gunned quite as fast.

Talk about how Barbie can go really, really fast in her super-short running skirt or how she tiptoes in order to spy on crooks. Show the child that a Teenage Mutant Ninja Turtle can cook meals and fall in love with another action figure he met at school.

With their big eyes, the Bratz dolls have X-ray vision and can see through anything. Spider-Man has been injured and needs to go to the hospital to receive emergency care.

Mix and vary the dolls and give all children dolls that are human-like, magical, and supernatural.

Collect a bunch of Barbie dolls (secondhand Barbies are perfect!) with different color hair, eyes, and skin. Dress them up in dresses, shoes, swords, factory work clothes, and capes. And there you have it: a game with more role models and more diversity.

Try to choose dolls that aren't the most extreme in terms of per-petuating gender stereotypes. There are all kinds of different dolls and figures available.

Barbie needs a sword! Princesses usually have swords!

Driving and Flying;
All She Needs Is Your Love

"I was looking for a birthday present for my nephew. I wanted to give him a toy that has to do with the home, since he likes doing the dishes and vacuuming. The problem was that all the vacuum cleaners came in pink boxes with pictures of girls on the outside, and he's big enough to understand that this means it's a toy for girls."

—MIKAELA, AUNT OF A FIVE-YEAR-OLD

"It's easier for everyone if the dolls are in one aisle, and Spider-Man and Star Wars are in another. That way, customers don't have to go on a wild goose chase."
"But why can't the Batman and Star Wars dolls be shelved along-side the other dolls in the store?"
"What? You mean, like, Batman would be next to Barbie?"
"Yes, wouldn't that make sense?"
"Haha! Not really, since Batman isn't a doll."

Thud! A toy catalog arrives in the mail. The kids devour it. *Vroooom!* There goes the car! But who's driving? The pictures show both boys and girls in the cars, but only boys sit behind the wheel. On the pages showing balls, there are ten boys and two girls. Among the water guns, there are no girls at all. Just to be extra safe, the different pages have different colors. On the pink pages, we have baby dolls, makeup, and brushes. On the gray-blue pages we have cars, construction toys, and guns. The packaging follows these color schemes and designs, too. The boxes for toys intended for girls often have rounded corners and come in bright, warm, often sparkly colors. The boxes with toys intended for boys come in dark, dull colors, with sharp corners and often some dangerous image.

To ensure the full distinction between toys for boys and toys for girls, the sales copy accompanying each toy is also gender coded. For the dolls, we have: *Just like a real baby! All she needs is your love and care!* The copy that goes with the cars says: *Drive it! Fly it! Fully controllable remote-control vehicle!*

The narrative governing what children can do and are supposed to do with the toys is set in place, and yet another opportunity for the children to let their imaginations run wild disappears. Instead, children are offered one-sided and ready-made stories about how they should be and play depending on what they have between their legs.

Girls who are pole vaulters, pilots, or mechanics rarely show up among products aimed at kids, and it's hard to find boys who take care of sick animals, grow vegetables in their gardens, or cook. The differences in toys result in children's imaginary lives playing out in different spaces: girls' lives take place in the home, and boys' lives take place out in the rest of the world. One consequence is that girls play in a more sedentary and calm way, and boys run around and make a mess. Boys practice their gross motor skills and courage, while girls practice their fine motor skills and ability to focus.

When I grow up, I'm going to be a boy!

How come?

Because I'm going to be a race car driver!

These different spaces affect how children practice creativity, how they learn to handle conflicts, and how they practice making and sticking to or breaking rules. To save the world, we have to be able to take risks and outsmart the enemy, which may require circumventing the rule book. If we're instead focused on taking care of dolls, cooking, and other more realistic activities, we need to be able to communicate and follow rules. We can't heat up the formula for too long, or else it could burn the baby. We can't put babies to bed with blankets over their faces, or else they can't breathe and will die. Children practice different kinds of fantasizing and different kinds of creativity in the two worlds, the world of boys and the world of girls. If, instead, all children can play in a world that is tied to reality but is also magical and supernatural, they will be better prepared to face the complex world ahead.

Suggestions

Try to give toys new meanings and introduce new environments. Baby dolls can be superheroes who search for a diamond hidden in the jungle or save the world from crooks and erupting volcanoes.

Try attaching several different meanings to the same toy. A stove can be used to bake cookies for a snack and to mix cement for the skyscraper under construction.

Encourage all children, especially boys, to play games that let them be caring, empathetic, and take up space in the home.

Encourage all children, especially girls, to play games that let them be technical, adventurous, take risks, and take up space out in the world.

Remove the packaging before you give a toy as a present. A stove can simply be a stove, not a "girls' toy"; a police uniform can simply be a shirt, not a shirt for a "boy police officer."

Have small children stay at home when it's time to go shopping for toys. Children are heavily influenced by toy placement and marketing in stores. When the children are older, you can discuss the toys and the messages being conveyed.

Bang, Bang! You're Dead!

"I read Spider-Man to my son, and Spider-Man was constantly being told that he was a coward if he didn't dare to fight."

—MARCUS, PARENT OF A FIVE-YEAR-OLD

"My daughter was pretend-fighting with another girl at preschool. They hadn't even wrestled each other to the ground before an adult

scolded them. But when the boys are pushing and shoving each other in the schoolyard, the adults rarely react."

—JOSÉ, PARENT OF A FOUR-YEAR-OLD AND A FIVE-YEAR-OLD

"I don't think pretending that he's killing others has a negative effect on him. It's just make believe."

—CAROLINE, PARENT OF A FOUR-YEAR-OLD

"I don't think playing war is a creative game. There's no saving lives and there's no hope. I don't want my grandchildren, whether they are boys or girls, playing war and having toy guns."

—BENGT, GRANDPARENT OF A THREE-YEAR-OLD, A FIVE-YEAR-OLD, AND AN EIGHT-YEAR-OLD

Bang! Bang! The bullets fly by. After a while a cry of triumph can be heard—*You're dead!* In Sweden, we haven't experienced armed conflict since the 1800s, yet playing war and other violent games is still popular among children, mainly boys. Or maybe that's why? Maybe the absence of war makes it simple and unproblematic to play war, lets us see it as one game among others?

Many of the toys aimed at boys are for playing war or some other kind of violence. Boys are taught to conquer, defend, and challenge by shooting, blowing up, and fighting. Violence becomes a method for achieving what you want. Through play, violence is presented as a solution to many dilemmas. These days, even Bamse, a Swedish comic book character and supposedly the world's nicest bear, is resolving more and more conflicts by hitting, blowing up, or hurling those who are mean or rowdy.

Many see boys' violent play as natural, while they think girls who play the same way are brutal, and they intervene to stop them. The rules of the game are entirely different for boys and girls. It's of course also very problematic if boys only learn one way of resolving conflicts, namely by resorting to violence.

Suggestions

Invite all children, and especially boys, to play games that are not violent. Weapons can be used as props in a store, and inventors can take them apart. Maybe the evil crooks are evil because they don't have any friends. Make soup with hand grenades, stir with the swords, and have a party!

Add a positive spin on killing games. Build an ambulance together that comes and helps the wounded. Take turns being doctors who save lives. Rebuild the city in ruins, with schools, grocery stores, homes, and other things people need.

Let all children try "evil" and "good" roles.

Play-wrestle with your children. This lets them challenge and be challenged physically. Since you—the adult—are there, they can learn where the limits are so that they don't hurt each other.

While playing, everyone, especially girls, can practice defending themselves in a positive way, both verbally and physically.

Choose toys other than weapons for your child.

Show children that conflicts can be resolved in many ways without resorting to violence. Play roundtable discussions, letting the children practice arguing and negotiating.

That's Not What Horses Sound Like!

"One day at preschool, my daughter was playing horse. The horses roared like lions and were pretty aggressive and loud. The teacher said: 'That's not what horses sound like, is it?' trying to get them to be quieter. But when boys are rowdy in the same way, no one says anything about it."

—PAULA, PARENT OF A FIVE-YEAR-OLD

"You really need to settle down. Can't you sit calmly like other girls?"

—KERSTIN, GRANDPARENT OF A FOUR-YEAR-OLD

The expectation that girls be calm, still, and quiet is pervasive. This leads to girls being admonished more frequently than boys when they are loud and take up space. That a cute girl with long hair can growl like a lion and become really angry is perceived as problematic in the same way that it's considered wrong for boys to be hesitant and shy, precisely because expectations are not met. But it's important to be able to say *no*, to practice taking up space and using vocal resources, especially for girls. Because if girls don't practice these skills, we risk reinforcing the patterns according to which boys are allowed to run wild and girls are supposed to be quiet and still. With respect to horses, in particular, maybe they don't make a lot of noise, but they can be both aggressive and threatening. The idea that taking care of horses is cute is another idea that needs reexamining. Although they may be pretty, horses are above all large, fast animals that weigh many hundreds of pounds.

When we let boys who are loud much of the time carry on, we're also doing them a disservice. Many adults stop listening to children who speak loudly or shout. Ears grow tired. And there's a risk that children shout more because no one is listening. It's a vicious cycle.

Suggestions

Allow all children, especially girls, to be loud and wild when they're playing. Have girls practice roaring like lions, running like big monsters, and using their bodily and vocal resources.

Have children lower their voices in regular conversations. You can ask, *Where is your volume button? Maybe on your ear?* Gently twist your own ear while lowering your voice. Ask if the child wants to try, too, and now you have a new game about voice volume.

When children are loud or yelling, try lowering your own voice and whispering to them. They will be curious and lower their own voices in order to hear what you are saying.

Kivi & Monsterhund (Kivi and the Monster Dog) by Jesper Lundqvist and Bettina Johansson was the first children's book in Sweden to use the gender-neutral pronoun *hen*. The publisher Olika released the book in 2012, launching a debate that led to *hen* being included in the dictionary of the Swedish Academy, in 2015. Learn more about *hen* on the podcast *The World in Words*, "The Three-Letter Word that Rocked a Nation" (PRI, March 26, 2018).

Once Upon a Time

"Of the 10 songs we sang, eight were about boys. When I brought this up with my colleagues, they thought I was being fussy."

—JOSEFIN, TEACHER

"Where are all the thoughtful and gentle boys in children's books? Is Alfons the only one?"

—HELEN, PARENT OF A ONE-YEAR-OLD, A THREE-YEAR-OLD, AND A FIVE-YEAR-OLD

"There's a girl on the cover. I don't want to watch that movie."

—SEBASTIAN, AGE FIVE

How do children catch a glimpse of the world beyond their closest family members? Through books! Children learn a lot from books, from the first board books and learning to recognize an airplane or a cat, to the longer stories and learning who is good and who is evil.

Books are and have always been an important way of spreading values, ideals, and ideas about the world. The stories influence and inspire our children and give them role models. Often, we may simply read children's books, without reflecting all that much on the content. But if we do, we'll notice that the protagonist is more often a boy than a girl and that most of the picture books reflect the patterns of traditional gender roles. There are many more boy protagonists than girl protagonists in children's picture books. Patterns in descriptions of boys and girls recur. Girls are passive, sensitive, tentative, kind, helpful, pretty, and proper, while boys are active, strong, brave, tough, short, or tall.

Books with boys as protagonists sell better, since both boys and girls can read them.

Fairy tales also gender emotions. Girls who face setbacks are terrified, sad, worried, or upset, while boys are frustrated, angry, or irritated. Animals like butterflies, birds, and cats are female, and more dangerous animals, like lions, bears, and tigers, are male. Women are very rarely thieves, and men are very rarely friendly fairies.

The places occupied by girls and boys in stories fit well with toy manufacturers' marketing. Boys are often out and about in the surrounding world, testing limits, while girls follow rules and exist in domestic environments. The gender trap in many stories is not only the uneven distribution of boy characters and girl characters, but also that the content so

A survey of children's books published in the US from 1900 to 2000 noted that each year 57% of books have male main characters and 21% of books had female main characters.
—Janice McCabe, et al., "Gender in Twentieth-Century Children's Books," Gender & Society, 2011

clearly shows that boys and girls are supposed to have different roles and characteristics.

In comic books, the world is even more starkly divided. Comic books aimed at girls have titles like *Barbie* and *My Little Pony. The Phantom* and *Spider-Man Kidz* are meant for boys. The extras that come along with the publications are gendered. Girls get jewelry and makeup, while boys get UFOs and water guns. In stories that at first glance may appear to be for all children—*Winnie-the-Pooh, Donald Duck,* and *Tom & Jerry*—the main characters are exclusively boys or men! Girls can be found in one supporting role or another, mainly as girlfriends of one of the main characters, or providing support with good food and beautiful smiles. This pattern is repeated in most children's shows and movies, too.

Books and movies are important because within them, children find inspiration for their games and role models for creating their identities. They affect a child's idea of what is feminine and masculine. By remaking and renewing patterns and narratives, we can use the power of stories and imagination to offer children more role models and thereby more ways of being in the world.

Once upon a time, there was a lady who wanted to travel into space.

But daddy! That's not a LADY! He has a mustache and a spacesuit. He's an astronaut.

Yes, but still. That's an astronaut-lady . . . with a mustache.

Suggestions

Talk with children about what you see in books and magazines and what happens in the movies. Tell them that the way things are can vary a lot, and that what is told or shown is just one of those many ways.

Switch *he* and *she*. Or use gender-neutral terms like *they* and see whether, and if so how, that affects the story.

Let Curious George become "she/her" and let space scientists be both men and women.

Replace the main character's name with your child's name. Other characters can have the names of other people in your family or your child's friends.

Draw and make up your own stories with your child. These activities will often turn into exciting adventures and creative images.

Choose a variety of books, magazines, and movies for children. This will give them a broader representation of reality and make it easier for them to see exciting role models with whom to identify.

Skip books and movies that convey skewed images and gender stereotypes.

	Girls/Women/ Females	Boys/Men/ Males	Gender-neutral
Main character			
Supporting character			
Characteristics			
Feelings			
Clothes and colors			
Jobs			

Conduct an analysis of your books. Use tables and fill in how many gender-neutral characters, girls, and women are the main characters in your children's books. Then do the same for the supporting characters, and note how girls and boys and women and men are described. The same kind of mini-survey can be done on movies and kids' shows.

43

Girl's Room, Boy's Room, Playroom

"My daughter always plays with the same toys. She will very rarely think to play indoor hockey but always has a great time when I get out the sticks and ball."

—CISSI, PARENT OF A FOUR-YEAR-OLD

"The more stuff he gets, the less his room seems to appeal to him."

—MALIN, PARENT OF A THREE-YEAR-OLD

A room is more than just a room. Different rooms invite us to do different things. A gym invites movement and action, while a classroom with desks and chairs invites us to sit down. Rooms can help children be creative in how they play and how they create identities, but rooms can also recreate stale boys' and girls' roles. The toys within a room and those that are kept out will influence how children play.

We often sort toys by appearance or by how they are meant to be used. Dolls are kept close to the stove, which in turn is placed near the doll bed, while all the different toys for building things are grouped together. Without intending to, we group toys the same way as in the catalogs. Parenting and interior design magazines show how beautiful rooms can be designed, as well as exciting rooms and cool rooms. We can often tell which ones are meant for girls and which are for boys. The girls' rooms have sheer materials and bright colors, while the boys' rooms are sporty and adventurous. But the features rarely address the skills, feelings, roles, and games the rooms inspire. Will a room encourage a child to be creative, careful, inventive, imaginative, crafty, organized, calm, or physically active?

Suggestions

Children will often start playing with items in new ways if the toys are moved around. Put dolls in the LEGO box, action figures in the dollhouse, and books in the random bin. The drill can rest next to the doll bed, and the Batman figures can live in the oven. They can make the bed and decorate.

Rearrange the furniture in your child's room. This can encourage new ways of thinking and playing.

Are the children having a hard time getting going with games? Remove a number of toys to give them more space and see what happens. Give their imagination more room to breathe.

Consider how toys are placed. Which ones are easy to reach, and which ones are in boxes high up on a shelf or in a closet? Switch the toys around every now and then.

Playing It Safe

"My daughter always receives soft animals and dolls, and my son gets cars and LEGO sets. I've told all our relatives that I want my children to get other stuff, but no one listens."

—LOTTA, PARENT OF A FIVE-YEAR-OLD AND AN EIGHT-YEAR-OLD

"I'd like to get Astrid a doll stroller when she turns two."
"That is very kind of you, Mom, but she already has one, and we don't have room for another."
"But that one isn't a real doll stroller. It's just a push toy for learning how to walk."
"It's great as a stroller, too."
"But Astrid and I have already picked one out for her."
"Mom, I said that she doesn't need a special doll stroller."
"Well, I know that girls really want those."

The presents are about to be opened. Everyone is excited! Everyone's eyes are sparkling with anticipation. When we give a present, we want the recipient to like it. It's a kind of affirmation. We show that we like the birthday child and can satisfy their wishes. Giving gifts is often as much about the giver as it is about the recipient.

Presents can be a sensitive topic and hard to address with family and friends, who generally give gifts because they like our children and want the best for them. Gender-stereotyped presents are often a way of playing it safe. Giving soft animals, makeup, or sparkly stickers to girls, and dinosaurs, LEGOs, or a remote-control car to a boy, that's a safe bet, right? When we're shopping for presents while tired or under a lot of stress, we readily reach for whatever's available. However, a child who already has five dolls or seven trucks is perhaps already an expert on playing with those and might appreciate new challenges.

Suggestions

Tell family and friends what kinds of gifts you want and need, so that the presents are appreciated.

If your child already has a bunch of soft animals, cars, or crayons and receives more of the same, ask to exchange the gift for something else. It doesn't have to be harder than exchanging an item of clothing that's the wrong size.

Presents don't always have to be things. Give experiences instead. Invite children to a movie night, a day of baking cookies, or a picnic in the park. Being together is special enough.

Give toys that encourage children to try activities other than those they usually engage in. Sparkly butterfly wings can be a big hit with a boy, and a whoopee cushion can make many girls laugh.

Dare to buy toys that the manufacturer has "coded" as girly for a boy and vice versa. Don't let the manufacturer's marketing department limit your options.

Wow! That's a Dragon Suit!

At a party, certain presents will evoke more delight from the adults than others. The more we *oooh* and *aaah* about a present, the clearer the message to children that this is something good and important that they should like. The crux is that we tend to reinforce and give attention to the things we expect that girls and boys will like, respectively. By offering positive, negative, or no feedback whatsoever, we show children what we approve of and appreciate, and how we want things to be. Few boys get to hear squeals of joy from adults when they open the arts and crafts kit, and few adults will prob-

Oh, you got a Barbie doll! She's so pretty!

48

Wow!
What a cool
Batmobile!

A puzzle.
That's nice.
Would anyone like
more coffee?

ably start in on the Play-Doh with the same enthusiasm as they might with a race track. Children can tell, very quickly, what the adults approve of. They also rapidly learn what to do and how to behave to get that approval. What we adults do or do not approve of doesn't just tell children what we enjoy, but also how we want our children to be—which indirectly tells them how we do *not* want them to be.

Suggestions

Having a chance to discover for yourself what's underneath the wrapping paper is exciting. Give children time and space to open presents at their own pace, and let them have that experience in peace and maybe a little bit of quiet.

See what happens if each present is affirmed as much or as little as the rest. How does that influence a child's experience?

If your child doesn't have time to open all the presents because the first one got all the attention, save the rest for tomorrow. This makes the celebration last longer, and your child can open presents at a comfortable pace.

All She Does Is Cook, Anyway

"We gave him a doll, a boy doll, no less. He played with it for a little while and then threw it on the floor."

—NOMI, PARENT OF A FOUR-YEAR-OLD

"When Smilla visits her grandparents, they always get out dolls and strollers. When her cousin Max visits, they get out the blocks. I'm sure they mean well, but it's a bit frustrating."

—GUSTAV, PARENT OF TWO CHILDREN

"At day care, they say that it's natural for boys to be loud and wild, that boys will be boys."

—FELICIA, PARENT OF A THREE-YEAR-OLD AND A FOUR-YEAR-OLD

"She received a whole box of LEGOs, but she just pretend-cooks with the pieces."

—CHRISTIAN, PARENT OF A THREE-YEAR-OLD

When we give children watercolors for the first time, we show them that there are brushes, water, and paper. We show them that the brush needs to be dipped in the water, then brushed against the color, and then applied to the paper. Certain things require preparation and an introduction; we simply have to learn how it's done. Even if it seems like girls automatically know how to play with dolls, and boys know how to play with cars, we're often ignoring the introduction to that playing that's been provided by other adults, children, siblings, or through various media. Although it's not always intentional, both adults and children are often quick to recreate narrow gender roles.

When new toys are given to children without an introduction, they will continue playing with them as they have been with other items. Children who play that they are taking care of and cooking for dolls and stuffed animals may use LEGOs as recipe ingredients. Children who are used to building

In 2015, Target announced that they would stop organizing toys and bedding by gender.

things won't see how plush toys fit into their games and will leave them off to one side.

When we try to broaden the scope of play for children and it doesn't work, we often see this as proof that their behavior is biologically determined and can't be changed. We underestimate the extent to which children, like adults, like doing what they know how to do and are good at. It's easier for children to build with LEGOs or do beadwork when they know that they're good at it. Being capable gives a sense of security.

Experimenting and trying new things can be scarier, since there are often clear rules about what counts as success and what counts as failure. Success is result-oriented, like creating a nice painting or being the fastest runner. But we can choose to see the ability to develop and learn new things as success. We can focus on a child's experience while painting, rather than the finished product, or on the feeling of running. This prevents children from being trapped in narrow roles, and lets them see ways of trying new things.

In general, we tend to notice and amplify things that confirm our own ideas more than things and events that challenge us. This creates a cycle of reinforcement. Those who believe that girls are genetically programmed to be more caring will probably notice girls more when they are playing with dolls than when they are playing with cars. Similarly, it can be easier to see the boys who are playing with cars than those who are stringing beads.

Suggestions

Spend more time introducing traditional girls' toys to boys and traditional boys' toys to girls. Tell them how the toys can be used or, even better, take part in their playing and show them.

Spend less time introducing traditional girls' toys to girls and traditional boys' toys to boys. Many others are already offering these introductions to your child.

There's a time and place for everything. Sometimes children aren't receptive to new toys or games. Wait a while and try again later.

Expand your own playfulness. Join in games that you don't usually play, or in games that your child appreciates but that you find tedious. When you do, you improve your understanding of your child's world and share more experiences inside it.

Look for girls who are playing games or doing things that you generally think girls wouldn't do. Do the same for boys. Use words to describe what you are seeing, so that these children's actions become part of your frame of reference.

54

Who Do You Have a Crush On?

"Today Leya came home and told us that they had been playing a game at preschool. They were supposed to say who they have a crush on. But Leya didn't want to because she doesn't have a crush on anyone. But her teacher got annoyed and said she should have just picked one of the boys."

—KAMRIN, PARENT OF A FIVE-YEAR-OLD

Many songs and games played at home and in day care or preschool are based on the idea that children are or will become heterosexual. In the traditional Swedish game *Bro, bro, breja,* the point of the game is to say who you like. And it can be a wonderful feeling, saying that person's name, sure, but why are girls implored to say "his name" and boys "her name"? When a boy is in the middle, the song goes "What's her name?" and when a girl is in the middle, "What's his name?" Many songs and games reinforce heteronormative values, and we sing along, without considering what we are really telling children.

What's happening in these situations is that we're implicitly assuming, in how we ask and what we ask, that the children are or will be heterosexual. It would be better for us to approach children with fewer preconceptions of this sort. A simple way of challenging heteronormativity is by leaving out the gender in these kinds of questions. "What's their name?" works perfectly fine in this kind of situation. "They" can refer to anyone and lets children choose freely how they want to answer.

Apart from that, we can also ask ourselves why it's so important to have a crush on or be in love with anyone at all? In addition to requiring that a child name a person of a specific gender, songs and games often impose the norm that we should be in love with a single person. This rule is based on the idea that love, or rather, *romantic* love, is limited to a single person. Hollywood and Disney like to stoke the flames of this idea, but what are we missing out on if we're taught to believe we should only feel love, romantic or otherwise, for a single person? Love can appear in many ways, and children are as open as we adults allow them to be. Children have no trouble being in love with several beings at the same time: their best friends, a hamster, and a grandparent.

Suggestions

Remember that it's possible to love several people and that children do not have to choose a single person. Love is a good thing.

Try replacing *her* or *him* with *them* in songs and games. Make a list of songs and games that are being played and check how many of them are heteronormative. Change the words so that everyone can feel included and recognized. Do the same thing for books and stories.

Explore which songs and games place expectations on children about being in love. Can the games be played in other ways? *Bro, bro, breja* can be played by telling the children that they can choose someone they like: an aunt, sibling, friend, or why not themselves?

In talking to children about liking someone, or about being in love or having a crush, use *they/them* to avoid assigning a gender to the person the child maybe likes, instead leaving the topic entirely open.
"I like someone."
"Okay. What's their name?"

Gender-Equal Play

How children interact with each other when they play, and with adults who join in their games, creates limits for what they can do, as do the things they play with, the materials those things are made of, and how the games are played. If we had gender-equal play—gender equality in playing and in games—we would simply have toys, not girls' toys vs. boys' toys. Stories and fairytales would be about all children, not just a select few, and all children would be allowed to set out on adventures in the home and out in the world. They would have opportunities to practice being independent individuals and caring relationship experts, breaking boundaries and following rules. While playing, they would be free to practice gross as well as fine motor skills, be free to wrestle with or hug each other. This equality in play would give children the opportunity to feel safe in many different roles and situations, and give them access to their whole imagination. Everything is possible in make believe. Babies can fly faster than jets, and Spider-Man makes delicious pancakes.

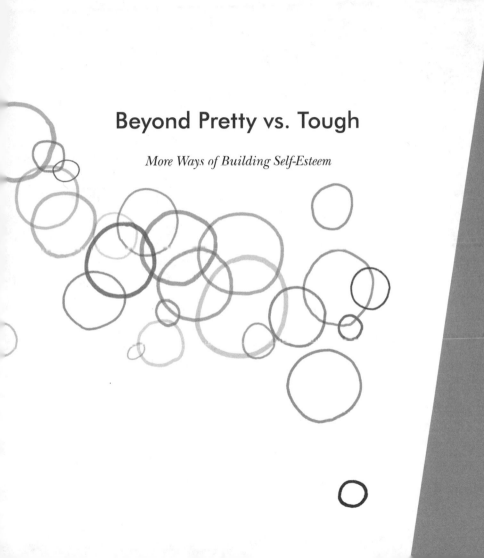

Beyond Pretty vs. Tough

More Ways of Building Self-Esteem

Happy Colors or Blue

"I like being able to tell the difference between girls and boys. I like buying blue clothes for my son."

—BRITT-MARIE, PARENT OF A THREE-YEAR-OLD

"My son wanted a pink shirt. I was worried he'd get teased, so I lied and said that there weren't any pink shirts, that they were all out. I bought a red shirt, instead."

—ANNIKA, PARENT OF A FOUR-YEAR-OLD

When the clouds part, and a spectacular rainbow appears, most of us are delighted and happy. The array of colors is incredible: red, orange, yellow, green, blue, indigo, and violet. Colors are exciting and elicit emotions. But there's a problem with the rainbow: the colors aren't for everyone. Already at the age of four, children are remarkably unanimous in asserting that pink is for girls, and blue is for boys. Walk past any playground, and you'll see this pattern. The children wearing blue, brown, black, gray, and green are most likely boys, and those wearing pink, purple, red, and yellow are very likely girls.

Strollers, blankets, and diaper bags fall in line with these gendered color rules. Girls' clothes and accessories have what we call warm colors, while those for boys are most often relegated to the so-called cool colors. Boys' clothes are also often drabber than girls' clothes, which are brighter and often feature white. Furthermore, girls clearly have access to most of the spectrum. No one would frown at a girl wearing blue or green overalls. But a boy in a pink coat or violet pants is a different story.

> Oh! You've bought a stroller already? So, you know if you're having a boy or a girl?

Perhaps we'd like to buy more colorful clothes for a boy, but that would require venturing into the girls' department, so the darker, colder colors will have to do. For adults, dark colors are often associated with status and power; they're official and professional. Men's business suits are seldom red, pink, green, or turquoise. Clowns, on the other hand, are always colorful. What values are we buying into for children? Do we think that children in clothes in warm colors and delicate materials are softer than those in cold colors and sturdy materials?

Decisions about colors have practical consequences, too. Dirt shows up more easily on light colors, which means that kids wearing light colors are expected to be careful and not get their clothes dirty. Clothes that are supposed to be durable—for instance, clothes for jumping in puddles or for crawling

Different colors have different connotations in different cultures. In the West, white stands for innocence; black is power, danger, terror, and evil; yellow and orange are energy and action; pink, white, and pastels are fragility; green is nature and the environment; blue is confidence and quality; red is action, passion, and drama.
—Marcus Jahnke, *Formgivning Normgivning* (Defining Form, Defining Norms), 2006

through the forest—are often made in darker shades. However, colorful clothes are a source of happiness, and they're easy to spot, which is a good thing in many contexts, not just on gloomy winter days.

Suggestions

When you're out shopping for clothes, try some new colors.

If there are colors missing in the boys' section, ask for more colors, or look for clothes in the girls' section.

Mix colors that are traditionally thought of as boys' colors and girls' colors. Blue with pink, black with purple, or green with orange and yellow.

Use fabric paint to decorate clothes with your child. Most kids enjoy making their own designs and using glitter and sequins.

Experiment with a color's *meaning*. Let pink and yellow be dangerous, adventurous colors, and have brown and black be gentle colors.

65

Dressing to Play or Dressing to Please

"Pull up your pants, Lisa. They look really good, but your bottom is showing all the time."

—JENS, PARENT OF A FIVE-YEAR-OLD

In Sweden, clothes are measured in *centilong* (cl). If an article of clothing says 110 cl, it's supposed to be made for a child who is 110 centimeters tall. However, a 110 shirt in the girls' department is often smaller than a 110 shirt in the boys' department. Does this mean that girls who are 110 cm tall are shorter than boys who are 110 cm tall?

Clothes for boys fit looser, too. They're made in sturdy materials and are often reinforced at the knees or elbows to withstand lots of active playing. Clothes for girls are often tight, fitted, and made from thinner fabric. Even denim pants are often fitted, with a low waistline. Matched with short shirts that only barely extend past the waist, these clothes constrain girls' movements. It's hard to climb and run and have fun if you have to fuss with and tug at your clothes the whole time to cover your belly or bottom. In the winter, it can get pretty cold, too.

Some of the major children's clothes manufacturers insist that fashion governs the differences between girls and boys; fashion makes girls' clothes so tight and fitted. Other manufacturers claim that they don't focus on fashion. Either way, when clothes that are meant for boys fit differently from clothes that are meant for girls, children don't have equal opportunities to be children, to move freely and have their bodies to themselves. Imagine if all children were allowed to wear clothes that are comfortable and kind to their bodies, and that are good for crawling, sneaking, running, and being mischievous.

Suggestions

Pick the style and material of an outfit based on what the child will be doing, so that you don't limit their freedom of motion.

For a looser fit, choose the next size up when you buy clothes in the girls' section. Shop for leggings for boys in the girls' department.

Set aside clothes that you don't think are good for your child.

A Skull by Any Other Name . . .

"Here, why don't you wear this Spider-Man hat, instead? Spider-Man is much cooler than Peppa Pig."

—MICKE, PARENT OF A THREE-YEAR-OLD

"We'll often tell a girl, 'What a pretty dress,' if she's wearing something nice. But we also really try to remember to tell the boys that they're wearing cool pants."

—ZAM, TEACHER

A few years ago, skulls were very popular on kids' clothes. In the beginning, the skulls were mainly featured on clothes intended for boys, but after a while they showed up in the girls' section, too. However, those skulls included ponytails and ribbons and bows. Apparently, the original skull and bones just wouldn't do. Clothes for boys often have a superhero theme or scary animals, or text that says *Boom!*, *Vroom!*, or *Bang!* The prints show action, something breaking or moving really fast. The images on girls' clothes are very different. There are cats and dogs, teddy bears and other animals that look nice and friendly, butterflies, hearts, flowers, and glitter. The images themselves are not the gender trap, here. Instead, the trap is how the two worlds are so very clearly separated, and how our children are being told they should be different from each other.

SYNONYMS

TOUGH – sturdy, hard, healthy, resilient, tenacious, rough, fierce, harsh, resolute, severe, merciless, demanding

SWEET – beautiful, kind, adorable, lovely, gentle, pleasant, sugary, appealing, ingratiating

NICE – likeable, friendly, good, neat, dainty, pleasant, polite, graceful

COOL – calm, cold, relaxed, level-headed, collected, reserved, tough, unmoved, awesome

✳ "Dangerous"

69

Different things happen to children depending on whether they wear a cute cat shirt or a shirt that has fire and monsters on it. Other children and adults approach them entirely differently in the two cases. It's not surprising that the responses to two distinct images would diverge. As adults, we know that clothes can evoke emotions, and that we can use clothes to blend in, to challenge, to get affirmation, or to be seen. Children with cats on their shirts are likely told that they look nice and that the cat is cute and cuddly, while children wearing monster shirts are likely told that they look cool and that the monster is scary. Children are assigned distinct characteristics based on the images on their chests. Boys are often dressed up for the part of being tough and cool, and girls are decked out to play nice and cuddly. A whole host of expectations are generated, and they're not always easy to live up to.

Suggestions

Switch back and forth between "tough" clothes and "sweet" or "soft" clothes, so that the expectations aren't so lopsided. This gives children a chance to be approached by others in more varied ways, too.

Combine traditionally gender-coded clothes in new ways. Match a pink dress with a pair of dark jeans or a scary T-shirt with a pair of tights with flowers.

Interpret the prints in new ways:
- *How does it feel to have a glitter dog on your tummy? Does this dog bite?*
- *How many skulls are there on your shirt?*
- *Batman looks pretty angry on your shirt, what happened?*

Use all the words—*sweet, nice, tough, pretty,* and *cool*—with all children. Mix it up.

When children are young, set aside the clothes that are most extremely gender coded. Children don't have ways of responding on their own to all the comments and appraisals made by adults and other children. When they're a bit older, they can object in an entirely different way if they feel that what's being said isn't right.

"You look so pretty in your dress."
"I'm not pretty. This is my superpower-dress."
"What a scary hat with that spider!"
"It's not scary. This is my warm-and-cozy hat!"

Awww, Look How Pretty You Are!

"Our daughter is always told she looks so nice when she wears a dress or has her hair up. By both of her grandmothers as well as other adults. Sure, our son gets to hear that, too, when he wears a dress and barrettes, but never otherwise."

—ANGELICA, PARENT OF A THREE-YEAR-OLD AND A SIX-YEAR-OLD

"She's already started trying to look nice and pick out clothes that she knows will get her the most attention."

—LINDA, PARENT OF A TWO-YEAR-OLD

"My daughter received a board book as a present; it was called My First Princess Book. *Almost every page asked the reader if the princess was pretty and whether her dress looked nice."*

—FREDRIK, PARENT OF A ONE-YEAR-OLD

"One cold day, my daughter had a total breakdown when I said she couldn't wear her dress. Gigantic tears rolled down her cheeks as she screamed, 'I want my dress because my teachers say I look nice in it!'"

—EMILIA, PARENT OF A THREE-YEAR-OLD

People respond to a girl in a dress. She gets to hear that she looks nice, pretty, and beautiful. The same thing happens when her hair is in braids or put up with barrettes, or if she wears a necklace. There's nothing strange about this. Dresses and jewelry are made in appealing colors and materials that attract attention. Adults are subject to this, too, of course. From the Nobel ceremony to the block party, dresses, not tuxes or suits, are discussed and assessed. The overall consequence is that girls, from when they're really young, receive a lot of affirmation about their appearance. Looking nice is linked to something positive; a pretty girl is a successful girl. Not being pretty and nice is, for many, the opposite, namely failure. Children who wear jeans and a shirt aren't subjected to the same kind of focus on their appearance as children who wear dresses. The crux is that children can't realize that the attention they get depends on what the person looking at them is feeling. They can't know that the positive attention associated with the clothes is not about *them*—nor do they understand that if they're *not* getting that attention, *that* isn't about them, either.

Clothes and appearance become important parts of girls' identities. The idea that a girl is successful if she is pretty makes many girls and women live with a constant feeling that they need to change something about themselves. This means that a fair amount of their time and energy is devoted to how they look. This obsession with looks teaches both boys and girls that girls are objects, things that are supposed to be nice to look at. Becoming an object to be assessed by

At the Opening Ceremonies for the Olympic Games in 2008, the organizers decided that the seven-year-old girl, Yang, who was supposed to sing, was not sufficiently pretty to make an appearance. Nine-year-old Ling was considered sufficiently pretty but not a great singer. The solution? Have the prettier girl lip-sync the better singer's beautiful singing.

others generates stress, which in turn can lead to illnesses, like anorexia and bulimia. By objectifying girls and giving them tight, fitted clothes to wear, we are also contributing to the early sexualization of girls' bodies. In 2008, the Swedish clothing chain Ellos tried to market a bikini for two-month-olds. Parents were quick to protest, and Ellos pulled the item.

Boys are not exposed to the obsession with looks or sexualization to the same degree. As of yet, no one has tried to market minimal, shiny Speedos for babies. Rather, boys receive attention no matter what they do about their looks. They are allowed to be active subjects. That said, satisfying expectations about being cool or tough or acting like a superhero is no walk in the park. If you're a boy, you might want to be cute every now and then, and have the niceness of your appearance affirmed.

Suggestions

Try to focus on how clothes work rather than how they look. Do the clothes feel good? Are they good for climbing in, soft to sleep in, good for sneaking around in, easy to run fast in?

Give all children opportunities to make themselves look fancy and play dress-up with glitter, gold, tulle, and loads of gorgeous colors.

Pay attention to other things about children—especially girls—than their clothes and how they look.

- *It's so nice to see you!*
- *How are you doing today?*

Take a STEM approach to the clothes children wear or how they have their hair. This shifts the focus from appearances and encourages children to think:

- *How long are those braids?*
- *How many dots are there on those socks? Should we count them?*
- *Is that the kind of scrunchy that can glow in the dark? How can we tell?*
- *How is that shirt put together? How are the sleeves attached to the rest of it?*

He Gets to Be a Little Bit Different

"I like the dress because it's so very nice."

—DANIEL, AGE THREE

"My younger son loves dresses. Both adults and other children react, but it's been pretty easy. People accept him but also make excuses for him, feeling the need to say that it's okay, it'll soon pass."

—JOLIE, PARENT OF A FOUR-YEAR-OLD AND A SIX-YEAR-OLD

"Lucas, hurry up and take off the dress. You know how angry your daddy gets when he finds you wearing it."

—ANNA, TEACHER

"At preschool, the teachers tucked my son's dress into his pants. They said it was getting in the way when he was playing."

—KAJSA, PARENT OF A FOUR-YEAR-OLD

"My son wants to have the same dress as his big sister. But I'm worried other children will tease him, and I don't know how to prepare him for this."

—ALLAN, PARENT OF A TWO-YEAR-OLD AND A THREE-YEAR-OLD

Today, no one bats an eye when they see a woman in pants, but 100 years ago, it was considered highly questionable. Meanwhile, both boys and girls wore dresses. Today, skirts and dresses are almost taboo for many boys and men.

Dresses evoke emotions, whether the person wearing the dress is a boy or a girl. Many parents reject dresses and glitter and flower patterns for their sons. They may be worried about their child being rejected, teased, or being called a "wuss" or a "sissy." Those words are sometimes used when boys transgress against gender codes and adopt something that, traditionally, is considered girly. Boys who want to wear dresses are more likely to be accepted while they're very young, because it can be seen as adorable. But as time passes, the pressure builds: boys should be boys and be dressed in clothes from the boys' department. Buying a shirt or a pair of pants for a girl in the boys' department is not at all as controversial. Being a tomboy is, for many, considered cool, something positive, linked to taking action. There's no equivalent term for boys.

At a deeper level, the fear of dresses and other traditionally "girly" clothes on boys is a fear of homosexuality. Stores that have tried to feature dresses or tunics in the boys' section have had to deal with upset shoppers, mainly angry dads.

Some of them are concerned about expected sexual orientation, that a boy who wears a dress or wants to have hair ties or similar objects will be gay. But, of course, dresses have nothing to do with sexual orientation, and their orientation should not affect how we treat our children.

Suggestions

Let all children try wearing dresses. It's fun to dance in a dress, and they're nice to wear when it's hot.

Give dresses new meanings. There can be strong dresses, brave dresses, sneaky dresses, fluffy dresses, and dresses for running.

Remember not to joke about children's clothes when they break traditional gender patterns.

Talk about cultures and places where boys and men wear dresses and skirts, caftans and kilts, for example.

Support your child if anyone is teasing them. Talk about how different people can have different ideas. Offer your child role models to lean on. This can be effective for all kinds of ways in which children can be challenged:

"That's for girls!"
"No, my dad has one."

"Only girls wear dresses."
"That's not true. Lots of boys wear caftans."

Affirm children's choices, letting them know that their choices are good and they are allowed to make them. Helping children be less dependent on what others think creates a more comfortable place in the world for them and gives them better self-esteem.

He Only Wants to Wear Scary Clothes

"He says he only wants to wear cool clothes. Black clothes or other dark colors. He likes shirts with scary animals, monsters, and skulls."

—ADIL, PARENT OF A FIVE-YEAR-OLD

"We try to mix it up, but she only wants to wear dresses. It's a battle we've just given up on."

—TOBIAS, PARENT OF A TWO-YEAR-OLD AND A FOUR-YEAR-OLD

"I usually bring my kids with me to the department store. I'll bring them right in between the boys' section and the girls' section, and then they can choose the clothes they want."

—JOHANNA, PARENT OF A TWO-YEAR-OLD AND A FIVE-YEAR-OLD

If children could choose freely, what clothes, colors, and other items would they wear? Do boys fundamentally dislike bright colors and red hearts, and do girls always want pink and glitter? Or can they ever actually freely choose? Children learn rapidly that clothes generate reactions, and that they can be key to positive attention. They know that they'll be told they look nice if they wear that special shirt. They learn that their friends will behave in a certain way if they wear those pants. Clothes can be a security blanket, a coping mechanism, an armor. Our clothes can let us feel a certain way or give us the attention we want. But it's not straightforward. If we pick the wrong armor, we could get left out. This makes most of us err on the safe side.

Different clothes let us explore different roles. It can be easier to feel bold and secure in dark colors and heavy fabrics, and it may be easier to feel small and fragile in light colors and thin fabrics. Learning to move in and out of roles, feelings, and characteristics is good practice for life. It helps us understand and feel empathy for other people and is a way for children to explore and understand what they encounter in their everyday lives.

Suggestions

Let children discover new clothes and new roles by trying on each other's clothes.

Make a dress-up box with old clothes, filled with pants, suit jackets, dresses, skirts, necklaces, and all kinds of shoes that children can wear when playing.

Introduce Playful Clothes Days by shifting the focus from the category of item to their color or some other feature: a red day, yellow day, monster day, or soft day.

One good way of cutting down on the drama surrounding gender-coded clothes is to let more children have access to them. Let all children try the color pink, for example.

Introduce a Hairstyle Day at preschool and let everyone try hair clips and fun scrunchies. Or a Mechanic's Day when everyone gets to try on blue overalls and use a wrench.

A Sock Is More Than Just a Sock

Most clothing stores for children are divided into a girls' section and a boys' section. This is either clearly marked or else it's implicitly clear through various color combinations or styles of clothing. This separation exists even for the youngest babies. A few years ago, in Sweden, the labels in clothes would also say "Girls" or "Boys," but most manufacturers have stopped doing that. When we talked to the stores, it became clear that they see the categories as something the customers want. Store representatives insist that customers are frustrated if stores aren't organized in this way.

Other incentives could include higher profits. When clothes are gender coded with colors, shapes, and prints, two customer groups are created instead of one, increasing demand. Fewer children can pass down their clothes to younger siblings than if clothes are not gender coded.

I'm looking for white socks for newborns.

I'd like to have this giftwrapped, please.

For a boy or a girl?

In 2018, singer Céline Dion launched a line of gender-neutral children's clothing.

Dividing clothes up into clothes for girls and clothes for boys, and displaying them in different departments in stores, reinforces the idea that boys and girls are, and ought to be, different. These days, there's a lot of talk about corporate social responsibility, which most companies take seriously. Social responsibility can pertain to how products are manufactured and transported, that dangerous chemicals aren't used, and that working conditions are good. Many manufacturers have added environmentally friendly or organic items.

But gender equality for children and children's equal access to colors, movement, and clothes that fit comfortably are not currently conceived of as part of corporate social responsibility. Many stores do offer gender-neutral collections in addition to their ordinary products. Gender-neutral products are a small share of the market but an important step in the right direction. A few manufacturers and stores promote gender-neutral clothing as a niche as part of their business plans. Hopefully more will follow suit. Wouldn't it be wonderful to simply have children's clothing, instead of boys' clothes and girls' clothes!

Suggestions

Make your voice heard. A conversation or an email from a customer can have a big impact. Stores are eager to please their customers. You can find contact information online.

Have young children stay at home when it's time to go shopping for clothes. When the children are a little older, they will have an easier time seeing how clothes are displayed and gender coded in stores.

If a store employee asks if an item is for a boy or a girl, you can ask why it matters and how the items differ.

Ask for ribbons in a mix of colors if you don't know the child's favorite color.

Look beyond the large chains. Many smaller stores and online stores offer gender-neutral clothing.

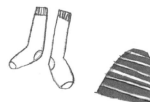

Would You Have a Look at Her!

"I just don't understand how they can dress like that! That's unbelievable!"

—PARENT, WATCHING THE EUROVISION SONG CONTEST

"She's almost naked! She looks, like, so trashy!"

—SIX-YEAR-OLD, WATCHING THE EUROVISION SONG CONTEST

When we feel free to comment on others or dismiss them by sighing or rolling our eyes, we are teaching children something. By constantly voicing negative opinions and derogatory comments about everything and everybody, we are judging people who aren't like us. Maybe we're relaxing on the couch, on our phones, and we'll say something negative about what someone has done or said, or, while reading the paper, we'll ridicule someone whose opinions are different from ours. We do this while we tell children that it's good to be a nice and kind friend. The negative comments made about girls and women are often about their looks. Over time, all children, boys and girls, learn that it's okay to judge girls and women by their looks.

It's not a coincidence that there are so many terms of abuse that are linked to women: *bitch, slut, hag, bimbo.*

The vocabulary is more limited when it comes to men. What we say and do affects how our children will behave. By making derogatory comments, we teach children that it's okay to say negative things about others and not respect those who are different. Making negative comments and claiming the right to judge others, these are the actions that lead to bullying. Preventing bullying is an active choice, not something that happens automatically. By letting negative comments go unchallenged, we are quietly accepting that it's okay to make such comments about others.

In 2017, 23.8% of girls and 16.7% of boys ages 12 to 18 reported being bullied at school.
—US National Center for Education Statistics

Suggestions

Instead of rejecting people who don't act like you or in ways you are used to, remember that people are different. We're not all the same. The word *different* does not mean good or bad; it just means different.

When someone makes a negative comment, follow up with a question. This makes the other person "own" the comment and explain their thinking.
- *How so?*
- *How do you know that?*
- *What do you mean?*

People are different!

Or just say:

"People are different! [In how they dress, look, think, what they believe, how they talk, or whatever the issue happens to be.]"

If someone generalizes about girls or boys, follow up with a question. It's good to take a closer look at generalizations.

"Boys are so mean!"

"Are all the boys in your group mean?"

"No, it's Lars, Björn, and Truls."

"What about the other nine boys in the group?"

"They're nice."

"So not all boys are mean?"

"No."

But That's How It's Always Been Done!

"We have to have a girl as Lucia. That's how it's always been done!"

—PRINCIPAL, ELEMENTARY SCHOOL

"We can only have one Lucia. The other girls are handmaidens, and the boys are star boys. That's how it's always been. It's tradition."

—CHORUS MANAGER FOR FOUR- TO SEVEN-YEAR-OLDS

Piller-paller, piller-paller, Santa's elves are tiptoeing about. Here comes Lucia, candles in her hair, and there we have her handmaidens, and the gingerbread cookies and elves. Right? Lucia is a Swedish tradition rife with gender-stereotyped roles. We're often told only girls can be Lucia and wear candles in their hair, or that there can only be a certain number of Lucias. The other roles are also divided by gender, so that only girls can be handmaidens and only boys can be elves or gingerbread cookies, or wear a cone hat and be star boys. Picking a Lucia can also turn into a beauty pageant, with the children voting for Lucia candidates. It's important to stop to think about the purpose of the holiday and the celebration, how the roles are divided up, and why. The Lucia holiday celebrates light. What could be brighter than allowing all

The Lucia celebration is an important cultural tradition in Sweden. Lucia brings light and songs into the dark Swedish winter and is celebrated in schools and preschools. The procession is made up of children singing carols. Once the singing is over, the audience will usually enjoy the Swedish *fika*: tea, coffee, and saffron-flavored buns. Conventionally, there was only one Lucia, and this role was played by a girl. Today, any child may want to be a Lucia.

children who want to do so to wear glitter or candlelights in their hair?

People often defend gender-stereotyped roles for the sake of "tradition." Traditions are simply things that recur repeatedly. For something to become a tradition, we have to take some kind of action to make that happen. That's why fairly new occurrences can become traditions. Halloween is a good example. We've only celebrated Halloween in Sweden for a couple of decades, but many people already think of it as a tradition. The meatball phenomenon didn't show up until the seventies, but many now consider it a necessary component of the Swedish Christmas smorgasbord. These days, many people choose to have veggie-balls instead, or other vegetarian dishes for the holidays, creating new traditions.

Traditions are linked to a certain time or era, and they change as society changes. When we challenge outdated gender roles, we need to take a look at the traditions that serve to perpetuate those roles, too.

Suggestions

Let children choose how to dress up for various holidays. Children are good at innovating, giving new meaning to old traditions and creating new ones.

Does your family celebrate a holiday that's not usually celebrated at your child's preschool? Tell the teachers so that they can celebrate more holidays and try new things!

Create new traditions filled with ideas you like! How about a One-Yard Day when your child reaches one yard in height, or a Picnic Day when the spring sun starts shining?

What's with all the blood!?! It's scary for the kids!

It's Halloween! It's tradition now!

Gender Equality of Appearances

We construct gender every day when we choose our clothes and get dressed. But gender equality of appearances is about so much more than being able to choose from an entire clothing store rather than just half of one. If we had gender equality of appearances, we could simply have *children's clothes* instead of clothes for boys and clothes for girls. All children would have access to all the colors of the rainbow, and to clothes that are comfortable and that are made for playing and being active. They would get to be tough and cute, look nice and cool, but wouldn't have to have certain kinds of clothes or attributes in order to "be someone" in someone else's eyes or to be included in games and fun. A dress would just be one clothing item among many others. If we had gender equality of appearances, all children would feel affirmed based on who they are, not their looks. They would know that they are seen for who they are and that we like them just the way they are. Friendly, funny, silly, or angry, it's all okay. All children would be received as people who think and feel and have the opportunity to build a strong and positive sense of self.

Beyond Taciturn vs. Polysyllabic

More Ways of Using Language

What's . . . *Ummmmm's* . . . Name?

You've just arrived at the playground, and you're just about to hit the swings with your child! You'd like to be friendly and say something to the parent and child who are already there. So, you're going to ask the go-to question: the name question. It's polite, not too personal, and all parents love answering it. Perhaps you can tell right away if the child is a girl or a boy: *Hi, what's her name?* But sometimes it's not that easy. You look for gender clues, but none can be found. If this is a him and you say "her," or vice versa, it could get awkward. For some reason, mistaking a child's gender can offend people. So, you try the stalling tactic: *Hi, what's . . . ummmmm's . . . name?* If you drag out the "um" long enough, maybe you'll get lucky and the other person will help you out with their child's name.

The gender trap in this everyday situation is that we focus on the child's gender, not the child. Is this due to old habits or do we simply lack the right words? The tricky thing is that the more times we ask whether the child is a boy or a girl, the more important the question seems to the child, to us, and to the person we're asking. As if it matters whether the child on the swing is a boy or a girl!

Suggestions

Say *child* instead of *him* or *her*, *boy* or *girl*:
- *Hi! What's your child's name?*
- *Your child seems so inquisitive!*

Say *their* instead of *his* or *her*: *What's their name?*

Come On, Girls! Hello, Boys!

We tend to label groups of children "boys" or "girls," in much the same way that we focus on the gender of individual children. When it's time to eat, cross the street, or get on the bus, a group of children will often be addressed by their gender. It's not as common for us to say, *Come on, all kids with long hair!* Or, *Come on, all short kids!* The problem is that when we label groups "boys" or "girls," we are once again telling children that this distinction matters, that they belong to two separate categories of people. There's also a risk that some children never or very rarely are recognized as unique individuals. Instead, they are one of the many in the anonymous group called *girls* or *boys*. This invisibility mainly affects children who are shy, timid, or quiet. Another kind of problem arises when we say *Boys! Settle down now!* when only two of the four boys in the room need to settle down. When we interact with children as a group and talk to them as a group, we often make them responsible for and blame them for something they haven't done. Children who get blamed via this kind of collective responsibility can be confused because they don't understand the connection between what they did and the reprimand. Of course, sometimes it's a question of misplaced praise, instead. We might praise the girls for having tidied up, even though only Sofia and Tyra did it. Maji and Lena didn't help at all.

Suggestions

A good way of avoiding collective blame and acknowledging each child as an individual is to say the children's names:

- *Majken, Elin, and Mirjana! Settle down now!*
- *Nice job cleaning up, Emil, Hugo, Karam, and Allan!*
- *Rosa and Fatou, we're eating now.*
- *Simon and Kim, hold hands when you cross the street, please.*

Skip the words *boys* and *girls*. Try using the word *children*, instead:

- *Do we have any strong children who can help?*
- *Look at the children! That looks like fun!*

Start using gender-neutral words. They give children more room to be and act, and they change the world.

CHILD (instead of *girl, boy*)

PARENT (instead of *mother, father*)

SIBLING (instead of *brother, sister*)

BELOVED (instead of *girlfriend, boyfriend*)

PARTNER (instead of *wife, husband*)

THEY (instead of *he, she*)

98

Are You a Boy or a Girl?

"My child wanted to have a new name, switching from Erik to Kimmy, and wanted to use they/them instead of he/him. The teachers were great. They simply let everyone know that Erik was now Kimmy and a them not a him."

—SARAH, PARENT OF A SEVEN-YEAR-OLD

"It's like, I feel like a them. It changes. Sometimes I'm a boy, sometimes I'm a girl, and some days I'm both."

—FRIDA, AGE SIX

Adults often divide children by their biological sex, as girls and boys. Children can be much more open and should be allowed to be open. As adults, we have to get better at asking children open questions, instead of assuming that girls look a certain way and boys some other. Girls can have short hair and wear a superhero shirt, and boys can have long hair and wear sparkle hearts. Ask children questions rather than assuming things.

When we meet children who don't fit our expectations regarding clothes or looks, it's easy to focus on that. For example, we'll say, *Wow, your hair is so long!* to a child with a typical boy's name. Instead of commenting on how a child is different from what we might expect, it's important to interact with them as we would with any other child.

In 2010, Sweden introduced a new kind of protection against discrimination: protection against discrimination on the basis of transgender identity or expression. The new law made clear that people, big and small, who don't identify with traditional gender roles are protected by the law so that they can be exactly the way they are without being discriminated against. This means that children can dress the way they want, use the voice they want, the body language they want, and choose the pronoun they prefer for themselves. More and more children are expressing themselves and changing their pronouns and names.

Our gender identity has to do with what gender we feel we are. It has to do with our heads, not what's between our legs. A child can feel like a girl, or a boy, or both, or something else. This makes the Swedish word *hen* (see page 38) very useful because it lets children choose their gender identity themselves. The word *hen* showed up in Swedish in the 1960s, but it didn't take off until after 2010. In 2015, it was included in the dictionary of the Swedish Academy, which now has three singular pronouns for people in the third person, instead of two! In English, the use of they/them as a singular pronoun is likewise gaining ground.

Sex and gender can be defined in various ways. Our *biological sex* is based on our sex organs, chromosomes, and hormones. *Gender identity* is what a person feels that they are. Your *gender expression* has to do with your clothes and appearance. Your *legal gender* is what your birth certificate, driver's license, or other official paperwork says.

When you're a cis person, your gender identity and gender expression are the same as the gender or sex you were assigned when you were born. A trans person might identify as a girl, boy, woman, or man, or as nonbinary. If you're nonbinary, you identify as beyond or between the binary gender norm, the man/woman dichotomy. Many trans people sense that their biological sex doesn't match how they feel beginning when they're young, in preschool. Previously, many people thought this happened later, in middle school or junior high, but that's not accurate.

Furthermore, some people mix up trans identity with sexual orientation. These are not connected. A trans person can be asexual, bisexual, heterosexual, or homosexual, just like a cis person. To whom we're attracted doesn't have to have anything to do with our gender identity.

Gender confirmation surgery (noun): any of several surgical procedures that a transgender person may choose to undergo in order to obtain the physical characteristics that match their gender identity.
—merriam-webster.com

101

India, Nepal, Pakistan, Australia, New Zealand, and South Africa are examples of countries that have introduced a third legal gender.

Suggestions

Getting used to something new always takes practice. Start using *they/them* pronouns if you haven't already done so.

- *Did you see the doctor? What did they say?*
- *Look at the baby! They look so sleepy!*

If someone changes their name, always use the name they prefer.

If you can't tell if someone is a him, her, or them, wait a little while, and maybe you'll find out. In the meanwhile, simply use the person's name, and you'll be fine in almost any situation.

- *Would you like to play with Liam?*
- *How is Liam doing? Is Liam eating chocolate?*

If you're not sure what pronouns someone prefers, ask.

- *What pronouns do you use?*

Pay attention to young children, too, and respect their feelings. Let them decide for themselves what gender identity works for them.

And This Year's Nobel Prize in Beading Goes To . . .

Often, we'll use different words to describe the same behavior depending on whether we're talking about boys or girls. While boys are inventing, girls might be crafting. Or we'll refer to girls as pretending while boys are constructing. Girls whisper; boys talk. And so on. The gender trap is that we use different words without realizing this, but also that these words come charged with different connotations and values. The words used for what boys are doing often express higher status. Inventions can change the world and are seen as technologically complicated, requiring intelligence and hard work. Crafting is a smaller, more temporary activity. You might craft something that's needed in the home or something that's meant to be ornamental. The goal is not to stake your claim to public space. Technology and construction are still coded as *for men*. And even though technology and logic are required for sewing, weaving, and knitting, these activities are often seen as crafts rather than technology.

These differences in values mean that girls and boys learn that what boys do is a little bit more important than what girls do. By extension, girls are seen as less important than boys. Not because what they are doing is actually less important, but because the words and values connected with their

SAME ACTIVITY
DIFFERENT WORDS!
blabber – discuss
skip – jump
giggle – laugh
be silly – joke around
test limits – disobey
fussy – careful
difficult – determined
whiny – sensitive

actions say that it is. This can also make boys not want to do crafts because crafting in itself is made into a "girl thing," not an activity that all children can enjoy. But don't most children enjoy painting, cutting out shapes, and pasting shiny sequins on fancy paper? Shouldn't all children have the opportunity to create things, large and small?

Suggestions

Try to go back and forth between the words you use. Say *hop* and *jump*, *giggle* and *laugh* to all the children.

Give the words new meanings. *Invent* stuff using crayons and scissors, and do *crafts projects* with wood and screws. See who can make the longest string of beads. Replace negative words: picky eaters are instead particular about what they eat.

105

Action Guys and Monster Dudes

"My daughter is almost three. She refers to everything as 'him.' Her teddy bear is a him, the doll is a him, the car is a him, the book is a him. I try to get a 'her' in there, but it's not easy. The word 'him' has stuck like superglue."

—ÖRJAN, PARENT OF A TWO-YEAR-OLD

If we listen to our own words and those of our children, it's easy to come away with the impression that there are many more boys and men in the world than girls and women. We often say *he/him* about figures, toys, and animals without realizing it, by default. Young children quickly adopt these conventions as their speech develops. Some people still use *he/him* generically: *If anyone asks, tell him we're in the store. He/him* is the standard, the supposedly neutral language. Consider the classic sequence of images showing primate evolution, from ape to human. The human is always a man. What would happen if we provided breasts and a vulva for the figures at the various stages of development? This idea that man is the norm and that woman

Here comes the dump truck. What's he going to do?

is something that deviates from this norm is repeated in our language. It affects our children and their perception of how much space they're allowed to take up.

Look at that wolf! He's so scary!

Suggestions

Switch from *him* and *her* to *it* or *them* for animals, figures, characters.

Try replacing *guy* with a less gendered word like *figure*, *thing*, *thingamajig*.

- *I like the figure you chose.*

Switch between *her*, *him*, *man*, *woman*.

- *Is the monster woman going for a ride?*
- *Wolves can be hungry. She could eat you right up.*
- *Let's make a snow-woman!*

Tie Your Shoelaces!

"The girls have incredibly sophisticated conversations when they're off on their own. They're really conversing. It's hard to believe that they're only three years old."

—INGRID, TEACHER

"I'm so tired of having to keep repeating myself. He never listens anyway. I almost always end up standing there yelling."

—ANTOINE, PARENT OF A FIVE-YEAR-OLD

"Boys can often be heard a lot and use a lot of sounds in their games. But if you take a closer look, you'll notice that there isn't much dialogue going on."

—KENNETH, TEACHER

There's no mistaking the joy when babies start babbling and understand that they can communicate with other humans in a more advanced way. All of a sudden, children can use words to express how they feel and can change their surroundings and experiences. But somewhere along the way something happens to their language development. Starting at a very early age, we adults spend more time communicating with girls than with boys, and when they're a little bit older, we often interact with boys with fewer syllables and short commands: *Tie your shoelaces! Come here! Put your jacket on! Wait!* We address girls with longer sentences and more reasoning and imagery: *Tie your shoelaces so that you don't trip on them and hurt yourself! Come here and put your jacket on so that you won't be cold out since it's freezing! Wait until I'm ready so that we can walk down the stairs together.* This may very well be due to our expectation that boys can't stay still for any significant length of time. Or, perhaps we think that girls are better able to understand words and language. Whatever the reason, after a period of time, boys end up with a smaller vocabulary. This can be seen in how they write when they start school. In general, boys write fewer sentences and have a smaller vocabulary compared to girls. This smaller vocabulary affects their performance in school, since many subjects depend on reading comprehension and listening comprehension. A rich language and vocabulary can help us appreciate new ways of thinking and new topics, and make it easier to understand and express our own thoughts and feelings and share them with others.

Because short commands don't require proximity, boys get less eye contact and interaction with grown-ups than girls do. Often, we won't expect any kind of response to those short commands, either. There's no dialogue. And it may be harder for us to get through when we call out like this, since the chil-

"Although gender differences follow essentially stereotypical patterns on achievement tests, for whatever reasons, females generally have the advantage on school marks regardless of the material."
—Daniel and Susan Voyer, "Gender Differences in Scholastic Achievement," *American Psychological Association*, 2012

dren might be lost in their own thoughts and not at all receptive. It's easier to ignore a reprimand that's simply shouted out than one that's delivered face to face, as part of a dialogue. When children hear these kinds of brief, impersonal bursts, it's easy for them not to pay attention. This in turn irritates adults who will then raise their voices. This way of communicating with (mainly) boys prevents them from practicing active listening, but we need active listening in order to understand others and cooperate with them. Children who have a chance to practice both speaking and listening have an easier time handling frustration and solving conflicts with other children.

Suggestions

Try to establish eye contact with all children and take your time when speaking with them. Avoid shouting out commands that land somewhere in empty space, leading to irritation.

Talk with all children, especially boys, and don't be scared of using long sentences and new words and expressions that the children don't know. Those kinds of challenges help them with their language development.

Set a good example and show that you can listen to what your child is saying. Children who aren't used to talking often need extra time to express themselves.

Clean your room!

I'd like for you to clean your room because there are things everywhere and it's almost impossible to enter.

Who Gets to Speak and Where?

"But the girls never say anything in class. They don't want to. It's just us boys talking."

—ANDREAS, AGE 14

"They say Ludde is so charming because he talks all the time, but that he needs to learn to wait his turn and not just start talking right away."

—LOTTA, PARENT OF A SIX-YEAR-OLD AND AN EIGHT-YEAR-OLD

Even though girls, on average, are taught a larger vocabulary and offered more opportunities to practice communicating, boys, as a group, dominate the speaking that happens in preschools and schools. The idea that boys are impatient and can't wait their turn is probably to blame once again. By offering eager children immediate attention, we achieve temporary peace and quiet. This will often be easier than helping them learn to wait. Impatient boys are often considered charming and driven. But while we attend to them, we're inadvertently telling those who sit waiting that what they have to say is just not as important. Boys are more often allowed to interrupt, too. Girls are assumed to be good at listening and waiting their turn, a turn that may never come.

Some people claim that women speak more at home than at work, and that they speak more than men altogether. Perhaps the lack of space for women to speak in public makes them talk all the more in private and makes young girls talk a ton outside the classroom but grow quiet once they're inside. Because we respond so differently to boys' and girls' abilities to listen and speak, children learn that boys' and girls' words carry different weight in various contexts. Children who don't live up to stereotyped expectations fare the worst. Shy, quiet boys and loud, impatient girls don't fit in. The ability to be a good listener is reserved for girls, and the ability to make your voice heard in large groups or public spaces is reserved for boys. Shared participation is important and is fostered by teaching all children to *make room* for others through active listening and *take up room* by expressing ideas and opinions.

Suggestions

Everyone has something to say. Ask shy children open-ended questions. That way, you're showing them that you are interested in their thoughts.

- *What are you drawing?*
- *What are you doing now?*
- *Where do you think the boat should go?*

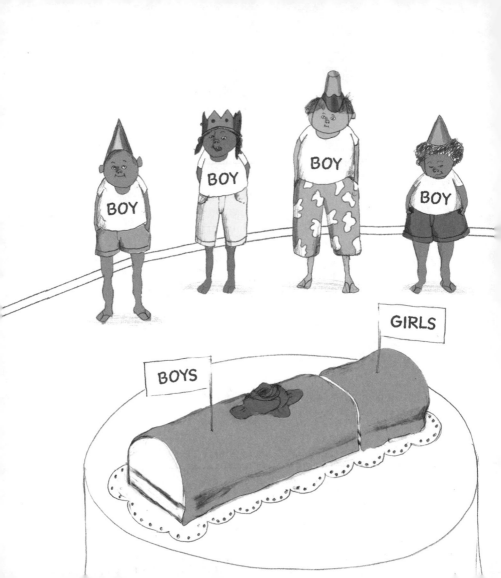

In school, the teacher uses two-thirds of the speaking time in the classroom. Boys take up two-thirds of the remaining time, and girls one-third.
—Eva Gannerud, *Lärares liv och arbete i ett genusperspektiv* (The Life And Work Of Teachers From A Gender Perspective), 2001

With children who have a hard time expressing themselves, ask fairly specific rather than general questions. Instead of asking them what they had to eat, try:

- *Of the food on your plate, which was yummiest?*
- *What color were the vegetables?*
- *Who else sat at your table?*

Instead of asking what your child did during the day, start by telling about your day. That way, you'll have more of a dialogue.

Talk to your child about what makes someone a good listener. Active listening involves maintaining eye contact, taking an interest, nodding, asking questions, and showing that you're engaged in other ways.

Listen actively to children who talk a lot, too. It's easy for adults to stop paying attention, but that can make the child talk even more.

Let all children practice not interrupting. At dinner, let everyone talk about something fun that happened during the day without anyone else interrupting.

Use a talking stick to organize talking in a group. Whoever has the stick is the one who gets to talk right then, and everyone else listens. The talking stick makes it easier for everyone to wait their turn and listen actively to the speaker. It also helps show that everyone's ideas and opinions are important.

Where Do You Live?

"Everyone, write your address on the paper."
"What should I do? I live with my mom and also with my dad."
"Well, write the other address over on the side."

There are forms to fill out for school. If you're lucky, there's room for two addresses, but often there's only space for one. That's because they're based on the idea that a child lives in a single place, which doesn't match reality today. In Sweden, about half a million children live in a situation that's different from the nuclear family (mother, father, child, all in the same household). More and more children have more than one address, and it's important that we show that that's natural. One way of doing that is by not assuming that a child only has one address and instead demonstrating curiosity about what a particular child's situation might look like.

Why don't your parents live together?

Why do your parents live together?

In much the same way that forms and address lists often only have room for one address, it's common for children who live in more than one place to only have information mailed to a single address. Whether it's information from pre-school, the dentist, or the doctor's office, it will often only be sent to one address. Even when communication works well between a child's separate households, sharing this kind information between homes is an unnecessary burden that single-address children never have to worry about. Children who switch households will often face a constant stream of questions about why their parents don't live together. This situation, the fact that children who are somehow outside the norm have to account for their lives in ways that others don't, is common. But what happens to children who constantly have to explain how they live, while others never have to? Constantly having to explain how we live creates a sense of being an outsider.

Suggestions

Show that you are curious and ask questions that aren't loaded:

- *How many places do you live at?*
- *Who lives with you?*

Let children draw and describe their families as part of getting to know each other. That will make showing their families into a nice and positive thing, something validating.

Practice asking questions about the kinds of things that get taken for granted, those that are seen as the norm. This can come across as a bit odd, since those kinds of questions are rarely asked. But it can show how often those outside the norm are expected to answer similar questions.

- *Why do you live together?*
- *Why are you having children?*
- *Why are you getting married?*
- *Why do you live in a house?*

What's Your Dad's Name?

"When my child and I were filling out the family tree at preschool it said 'Mother' and 'Father.' Same thing with every form we had to fill out. I had to cross out the labels and write 'Mom 1' and 'Mom 2.'"

—REBECKA, PARENT OF A THREE-YEAR-OLD

"We were talking with the kids at lunch. They asked each other what their fathers' names were. Liv said she didn't have a dad. One of my coworkers said: 'What? Did your dad die?' Liv was very confused because she has two moms."

—SAMIRA, TEACHER

Questions may be asked with the best of intentions, but they can turn out very wrong. That's because we have a traditional image of what a family looks like, and that image hasn't caught on to the fact that society has changed. This situation leads to the effective erasure and exclusion of many children and their families. We still talk of parents who live with their child but not with a partner as "single parents," even though they may be co-parenting with several other people. This

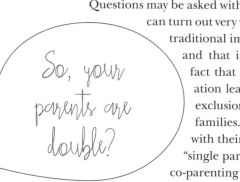

So, your parents are double?

120

expression stems from an era when it would be much more common for a woman to be the only caregiver.

Today, things are different. Even if a child lives full time with one parent, other parents may also have custody and shared responsibilities. Being a parent is something you keep on being, no matter where your children live.

In Sweden, forced sterilization was legal until 2013. Before 2013, anyone who wanted to have a gender confirming procedure or change their legal gender had to agree to being sterilized. Now, people who want to change their bodies so that they better match their gender identities can decide for themselves if they want to have the chance of having biological children. This means, among other things, that more and more people who identify as men and look like men will be pregnant.

Donor

What's your dad's name?

Precisely because there is so much more variety in family configurations these days than, say, 20 years ago, we need to start asking questions in new ways, not load them up with assumptions. One way is by asking about relationships instead of relatives. A woman who picks up a child at preschool or at the playground doesn't have to be the child's mother. Maybe she's the mom's or the dad's new partner? Or maybe she's a friend. By asking open questions we display curiosity without ranking families as better or worse than others, and we demonstrate that we know that families take different forms. This lets all children and their families feel included.

Suggestions

Practice asking questions that are more open and less loaded. Adopt the mindset of not knowing but being curious and wanting to know.

- *What is your parent's name?*
- *How many parents do you have?*
- *Is that your parent?*
- *Who is that?*

Use the word *parent* instead of *mom* or *dad* to make it easier to be inclusive.

Gender Equality Through Language

Language is a subtle but strong influence. Depending on how we talk with our children and the words we choose, we can either reinforce roles and patterns that limit them or challenge that framework and give them a richer reality. It may seem like a small thing, changing certain words and adding others, but in the long run it can make a big difference. If we had gender equality in and through language, children would have access to all the magic of the alphabet and its words. Children would be addressed as individuals, and their various activities wouldn't be diminished through a choice of words. *Them*, *him*, and *her* would all be equal. Children would have the opportunity to develop rich vocabularies and practice putting their ideas and feelings into words. All children would be able to practice making themselves heard without necessarily speaking over anyone else. In their interactions, listening actively and speaking would be equally important and natural. Gender equality through language would let us see the children behind the words and give them the freedom to express themselves, to participate, and to influence their own lives.

And They Played
Happily Ever After

More Ways of Being Friends

The Boys Are Over Here!

"My son was friends with both girls and boys at day care. But right around when he turned three, girls and boys stopped playing together. And no one seemed to think it was weird."

—MARCUS, PARENT OF A FIVE-YEAR-OLD

"When my son listed the names of the other kids at school, he mentioned Noel, Karam, Mohammed, Kasper, Emil, Björn, and Petter. You'd think he went to an all-boys school."

—RITA, PARENT OF A SIX-YEAR-OLD

You're about to drop off your child at day care. It's been a somewhat stressful morning, and finally your child's shoes, coat, and hat are all where they're supposed to be and you're on your way. When you get to the day care center, Solveig, the teacher, says, *Hi, Philip! I'm happy to see you. Let's go see what the other boys are doing!* She acknowledges Philip by saying his name and then introducing him to what is going on. Everything's done out of thoughtfulness for the child and for you, so you can get to work on time. However, what also happens in this everyday situation is that gender categories for friendships and playing are being created. When we thoughtlessly say, *Here are the boys* or *Here are the girls*, we tell children that gender matters and that girls are supposed to play with girls, and boys with boys.

Suggestions

Make all children potential friends:
- *Here's another buddy!*
- *Come, let's go play with the other kids!*
- *Let's go and play with all your friends!*

Talk about the activity instead of the gender of those doing it:
- *Here are the soccer players!*
- *Here's the art crowd!*
- *Here are the splashers and swimmers!*
- *Here are the building buddies!*

Refer to all the children by their names instead of as *girls* or *boys*. This shows them that they are all potential friends and interesting to play with.

If the staff at your child's day care center or preschool routinely suggest that girls play with girls, and boys with boys, talk to them about it.

128

Oh, They're So Cute!

"Teo was so cute when he was playing with Lisen. He pushed her against the wall and tried to kiss her."

—SUSANNE, PARENT OF A ONE-YEAR-OLD

"My little Astrid is Ludde's future wife."

—DENAIDA, GRANDPARENT OF A ONE-YEAR-OLD

"They've been best friends since they were two years old. When they started school, they got teased for being in love. Now they don't play with each other until after school. Mia has other friends, but Viggo is all alone during recess."

—PETER, PARENT OF A SEVEN-YEAR-OLD

Two boys or two girls who are best friends rarely get asked if they're in love or whether they're going to get married when they grow up. But boys and girls who play with each other are often told how cute they are together. The trap we fall into is labeling their friendship as romantic love. In general, adults expect children to be heterosexual. This influences ideas about friendships and makes it harder for boys and girls to play together. By the age of four, most boys and girls already know who is "supposed to" be friends with whom and how

Heteronormativity means that everyone is expected to be heterosexual. *Masculine* and *feminine* are conceived of as opposites, which means that inequality is considered natural. Heteronormativity reduces gender equality to statistics—the number of women and the number of men. Heteronormativity affects pretty much everything in our lives, for example our conceptions of friendship, family, and love.

129

they are supposed to act toward each other. Heteronormativity means that girls and boys are supposed to play apart. Children who are friends with someone outside their gender have to figure out how they're going to handle that and explain to the rest of the world that they're not in love, they're "just" friends. Children who play inside the gender lines don't have to worry about this. When adults try to fit children's friendships into adult preconceptions about heterosexual love, children lose a lot of friends. Having to give up a close and dear friend just because of their gender can be very hard.

Suggestions

Interpret children's close friendships as love, not romantic love.

Show children that friendship and love can take many forms. Girls and boys can be friends, boys can be in love with boys, and girls can be in love with girls.

Present them with a variety of friendships and ways of loving, for instance by reinterpreting fairy tales and other stories. Let Cinderella be best friends with the prince or let her fall in love with another princess.

Let children express their feelings for their friends using their own words.

It Was His Fault!

"I don't want Agaton and Eskil to play with each other. Eskil always has them breaking stuff and drawing on the walls, and he always wants to be the boss of everything."

—JOHAN, PARENT OF A TWO-YEAR-OLD AND A FOUR-YEAR-OLD

"At home, my son gets more negative attention, even though I really try not to get angry when he's emptied the soap bottle all over the bathroom for the hundred-millionth time."

—HELEN, PARENT OF A ONE-YEAR-OLD, A THREE-YEAR-OLD, AND A FIVE-YEAR-OLD

"Your son spends a lot of time teasing other children. He's always ruining things for the others when they're playing."

—ANN-CHARLOTTE, TEACHER

"Boys fight and ruin stuff. They're not fun to play with."

—YASMIN, HEDDA, AND FELICIA, AGE NINE

The idea of boys as mischievous and rowdy is often a self-fulfilling prophecy. The image is based on our expectations that boys are physical, wild, mischievous rule-breakers. One consequence is that boys often feel that adults side with "the

In addition to the fact that boys come to school on average having more problems, they also get penalized more for having these behaviors.
—"Boys Bear the Brunt of School Discipline," *US News*, 2016

131

girls," and that no matter what happens, boys are always blamed. We adults will often assume we know what's happened and who did what. The image of the rowdy boys is reinforced by boys generally receiving more negative attention than girls: they are told what they're not allowed to do or what they shouldn't have done. It's also very common for one or two boys to be blamed for everything. Boys who are often mischievous and break stuff are blamed for one thing after another, even if they had nothing to do with it. In those circumstances, those boys stop listening to what adults say and adopt the mantra *It wasn't me!* They use this to try to protect themselves against all the negative attention. Another way they try to handle the negative role adults assign them is by trying to make being rowdy and not listening to adults into something cool.

The image of boys as wild and misbehaving is something that all children need to figure out how to deal with. Many girls don't want to play with boys because of this negative image. Landing the role of rowdy destroyer-of-stuff and having to live up to it isn't much fun.

Research suggests that children younger than 11 don't learn from reprimands. Their brains are made to learn from success, not failure.
—Anna C. K. van Duijvenvoorde, et al., "Evaluating the Negative or Valuing the Positive? Neural Mechanisms Supporting Feedback-Based Learning Across Development," *Journal of Neuroscience*, 2008

Aggressive self/destructive behavior in children and teens should always be interpreted as an invitation. The child is inviting you to help them change something because they're not okay.
—Jesper Juul, *Aggression: Ett Nytt Och Farligt Tabu* (Aggression: A New and Dangerous Taboo), 2014

It wasn't me!

Suggestions

Replace *don't*, *can't*, and *no* with words that describe what you *do* want the child to do. That way, you're offering children an opportunity instead of a constraint.

Instead of: No, don't climb out the window.
Say: If you'd like to go out, please use the door.
Instead of: You can't run across the street.
Say: You can skip or walk here, next to me.

By replacing *no* and *don't* with opportunities, you can avoid a lot of nagging, and when you do need to use *no* and *don't*, the children will have a better chance of hearing you.

Point out when children, especially boys, are kind, helpful, and friendly.

Help children who are often rowdy find a new, more positive role to play by assigning them the responsibility of helping a younger child or taking care of an animal or an imaginary friend.

Invite children who act disruptively to take part in games. Talk about what they're doing instead of blaming them for it.

Adam and Minna are sad when you kick apart the stuff they've built. Come, let's help them build it even bigger.

If a child it stuck in a negative role, give them an imaginary friend who can absorb the negative attention and let the child be the problem-solver.

Here we go again. Little Monster has been drawing on the wall. How can we make Little Monster understand that we draw on paper, not on walls?

Let children be part of figuring out what to do about situations they've created. That can reduce the sense of guilt and help them find a more positive role and take responsibility:

What you did with Nils' hat wasn't funny. No one is allowed to throw anyone else's hat in a puddle. What can we do now to make things better?

Let the children explain what happened. That helps make a child's thoughts clear so that you can notice them instead of your own assumptions. Ask open, not loaded questions.

- *What happened?*
- *What were you thinking at that point?*
- *How did that make you feel?*
- *What can we do now?*

Make sure that no child receives too much negative attention, especially not boys.

Introduce "Yes Rules" that say what we're allowed to do instead of rules that only say what's not allowed. Talk with your child about the "Yes Rules" that apply at home, at preschool, and other places.

Now They're Wrestling Again

LGBT people are more likely to be targets of hate crimes than any other minority group.
—*New York Times*, 2016

Simon is grabbing Niklas roughly around the waist and trying to push him over. Or perhaps Simon walked up to Niklas and is giving him a super-big hug, almost knocking them both over? When very young boys hug each other, everyone thinks it's very cute. But as they get a little older, the hug transforms into wrestling or rowdiness. Men rarely hug, and when they do it often involves slapping each other's backs.

Strict gender codes tell us how we're supposed to express affection with our friends. Boys have to make do with pushing each other to show affection. Hugs and other signs of intimacy are reserved for girls. Ironically, boys are often very close to each other during sports and showering. In those contexts, derogatory jokes about gay people and old ladies serve as proof of being a "real man" who takes a clear stand against femininity and homosexuality in order to fit some notion of what a man should be. But don't boys need to feel closeness, too? What happens to boys who never get hugged?

You're so touchy-feely!

135

Suggestions

Have hugs be part of friendships and let all children be friends.

Model good friendship behaviors by being close with your friends.

Let all children experience positive physical contact and encourage intimacy among all children, especially among boys.

Give stuffed animals traditional boy names and show that they like to cuddle.

Giving and receiving massages is a good way of learning positive physical contact. Through massage, we practice touching somebody else in a soft and comfortable way, and we learn how to express what feels good or not for us, too. Plus, massage helps us relax and satisfies our need to be close to someone.

The Law of the Jungle

"The boys race to be the first one out on the playground, the first one in after break, and the first one to get their bike or snack, or anything. It's extremely tiresome."

—ULLA, TEACHER

"Greger is always driven to get ahead of his big sister. He's incredible, a real mini-bulldozer."

—TOBIAS, PARENT OF A TWO-YEAR-OLD AND A FOUR-YEAR-OLD

Who's the strongest? Who can jump the highest? Knowing who is the tallest, strongest, and best is part of the idea of men's friendships. From a young age, boys are seen as competitors who like to challenge themselves and others. Rarely are the competitions about who can draw the best or be the best buddy. The focus is often on physical activities and on being brave. This conception of boys' friendships also includes the idea that they like to spend their time in large groups. Playing in large groups has benefits, because the

Let's
get 'em!

children get to practice getting along and, ideally, expressing themselves in a large group and listening to others. A big group allows for community and provides context. It also offers the opportunity to practice competing, which can be positive for creativity and personal development.

Often, adults won't participate in boys' games in the same way they do with girls. Boys will often play at a greater distance away from adults. This becomes very clear in preschool, when girls will often play right where the adults are, and the boys play without adults observing them. This means that boys often have to negotiate their rules entirely on their own, which in turn means that brute force will often rule: the loudest and wildest boy gets to decide. Being able to claim space and to challenge others are important skills, but not when there's nothing to counterbalance them. Practicing getting along and collaborating is just as important.

The idea that men and boys are blunter in how they communicate with each other and therefore have an easier time handling conflicts is a myth. Being blunt is supposed to mean being clear about what you think and feel. But when the law of the jungle applies, there isn't much space for personal opinions, which means that straightforward and honest communication is not easy at all.

Changing rules or roles within the norms of a group is one thing; suggesting entirely new rules and trying to change one's own role within the group is another. Those who try to challenge the group or who don't live up to the ideals and norms in place are most often made to conform. Boys show each other what's what by physically hurting each other or by teasing and laughing at those who don't abide by the norms. The stronger the peer pressure and the hierarchy, the harder it is to challenge the group's ideals and norms. Getting personal isn't part of the image of boys' friendships. Instead, boys are expected to keep a certain physical distance from each other, and a certain distance from their own feelings. Displaying signs of vulnerability in front of the group is taboo, so it's important to stay in control, and not let your emotions show, to fit the image of a "real boy." Once they reach a certain age, children punish departures from the boy norm using expressions along the lines of *What are you, a girl?* and *You cry like a girl!* Boys learn to stake out their identities at an early age by saying that they are not girls, or by rejecting things that are considered "girly." Denigrating girls and what girls do becomes part of being a boy.

Distancing yourself from what is considered girly is an important aspect of masculine community.
—Yvonne Hirdman, *Genus: Om det stabilas föränderliga former* (The Mutable Shape of the Immutable), 2002

Suggestions

Boys are told by so many sources that they should compete with each other and challenge each other. Help them have access to games where they don't have to do that, and highlight features other than competition when boys play.

- *What a great pass he made. He must be very responsive!*
- *What a nice pit you have dug together!*
- *You are so kind to Jonas!*

Play with boys and practice getting along and interacting. Cook food or bake together. Give children, especially boys, opportunities to play in pairs and small groups.

Encourage all children to find their own path and be their own Pippi Longstocking.

Explain that being like everyone else is not a requirement. It's fun and exciting when people are different.

Encourage games that enable collaboration. Award points for passes rather than goals scored. Award points for helping a friend rather than for finishing first. Do baking projects and see how long you can make a snake of dough if everyone helps out.

Have children compete against themselves rather than against each other: How fast did you run today? Can you run even faster tomorrow?

Give your child a little sensitive figure who is afraid of not winning, afraid of not being good enough, afraid of monsters under the bed, and so on. Your child can help the little figure overcome their fears; this can help children who feel they aren't good enough.

Playing in Pairs

There's another myth and gender trap having to do with friendship, and that's the notion that girls are better off playing in pairs. If there are three of them, one will be left out, or maybe have to be the dog, when they play house. Playing animals can be a lot of fun, but not when it's a way of signaling that someone has a lower status or that someone isn't really allowed to be part of a game.

Playing in pairs often has benefits because children have a chance of practicing close interaction. They practice listening to each other, caring, negotiating and compromising, and being flexible in a close relationship. This creates a sense of security and closeness and helps with language develop-

ment. But adult expectations about girls not playing well in threes also limits them. Girls who play together in pairs are careful to be similar to their "best friend." The security best friends feel is based on a sense of belonging that in turn is often based on similarity: no one stands out or is different.

This makes girls who play together a lot develop a habit of trying to control each other. Another consequence of the twosomeness is that girls conceive of competition as something negative. Competing with each other poses a risk to the strong twosomeness. Many girls handle this by saying that competition isn't important or that they don't care about winning. We adults nod approvingly, since it matches our preconceptions about girls not being competitive. Competition is based on the idea that there's a variety of opinions and characteristics among those who participate.

Preconceptions about girls also include the idea that they're good at gossiping behind each other's backs. It wouldn't be surprising if this were actually accurate, given that the concept of friendship is based on being used to having one person all to yourself and your similarity with that person. Under those circumstances, any influx of people or any other way of being poses a threat. Saying mean things about someone becomes a way of shoring up the defenses that protect a pair and its twosomeness, and of keeping others out. The importance of being alike makes conflicts unpleasant because they threaten the closeness of the two girls. In much the same way as the law of the jungle, the world of best friends creates fixed roles and clear rules. Just because everything seems to be going smoothly doesn't mean that everything is just fine and perfectly equal. One child may play the leadership role the whole time, or be the creative one, or the funny one, or the one who always follows along and adapts. The opportunities for practicing different roles and trying on new characteristics are limited in much the same way as under the rule of brute force.

No, it's not a game—we're just kicking the ball around

Suggestions

Encourage girls to play in groups of three and in larger groups. Have two friends over for a playdate instead of one.

In the US, 54% of business owners are men and 36% are women. (The remaining 10% are male/female owned or publicly held.) —US Census Bureau Survey of Business Owners, 2012 statistics, published 2017

Encourage all children, especially girls, to compete with and challenge each other. It's fun and increases independence.

When girls start talking about best friends, explain that it's possible to have several best friends and many different buddies. With some friends, it might be fun to climb trees, with others it might be more fun to play games.

Take an active role in supervising children when they play. If a child is excluded or often seems stuck in the same role, join in and top off their creativity with some new ideas. A "dog" can instead be an aunt who has just returned from a trip, and a "baby" can be a scary monster breathing fire. Explain to your child that conflicts are a natural part of human interaction; they arise because we're all different, and we have different ideas and feelings. Since we can't read each other's minds, conflicts will arise. Conflicts aren't dangerous; we can think of them as a way of finding out about our differences.

Let all children, especially girls, practice making their own choices. Ask every child what they want to do and let them practice explaining their choices.

- *What is good about your choice?*
- *What are you thinking right now?*

Use the word *different* often and in positive contexts. That helps show your child that diversity is good and doesn't have to be scary.

- *Look how different they are!*
- *Look, you have two different gloves. Fun!*
- *There's no right way. Some people like to sleep with a blanket and some people like to sleep without.*
- *You can do it your way, and I'll do it mine! Yay!*

I'm Not Welcome

"I can tell that Tim wants to play with the girls, but he doesn't really seem to know how to approach them."

—JENNY, PARENT OF A THREE-YEAR-OLD

"Rosa often says that the boys won't let her play with them. Even though the adults have told them to include her, they still won't."

—DARKO, PARENT OF A FOUR-YEAR-OLD

"We don't want to play with boys. They don't know how to play."
"But you play with Sebastian. He's a boy."
"But we just play monsters with him. Girls play harder games."

Many games have subtle rules that can be hard to spot, secret codes for how to gain access. The trick may be knowing how to play or what the purpose is. Sometimes, the secret code is very strict and limited; sometimes, the game is more welcoming and open. In some games, children are supposed to ask if they can join, be assigned a role, and then start playing. In other games, they have to bring something in order to be able to play, and in some, you just kind of shout out and join in. Children can also come up with their own roles and step into the imaginary world of the game. For adults, we talk about social competence and the ability to read a room or know what's appropriate in various contexts. It's not that easy for children. Those who don't know the invisible rules or aren't that good at reading them often don't understand what they're doing wrong and why they're being excluded.

Meow, can I play?

When we claim that children choose their own playmates and their own games, we step into a trap. We can't see that we're not providing them with the same opportunities to play with each other. The more gender-segregated their playing, the greater the likelihood that they will develop distinct sets of rules and norms for how to play. It's easy for them to get stuck in limited roles and assume that playing has to be done the way they're used to. This makes them less able to get to know others and find new friends.

Suggestions

Let children have friends outside of preschool. Your child's BFF from preschool doesn't have to come along for swimming lessons. There will be new friends to make at the pool. Being a part of multiple social contexts is a good thing: it lets a child try out a new way of interacting.

Friends don't necessarily have to be other children. Adults, animals, and imaginary friends are good candidates, too.

If your child has a hard time approaching other children, talk about how there are different ways of becoming friends, and that it's okay to experiment. Sometimes, it works to simply start playing next to someone or to walk up to them and say, *Hi! Do you want to play with me?* At other times, a child will need to have figured out a role for themselves in order to join. Practice these different scenarios to minimize any drama and give your child the confidence to try it out for real.

But We're Just Playing Around!

"My child spends the whole day at preschool scared of being drawn into a 'play-fight.' But he says he's afraid of saying no, too."

—VLADIMIR, PARENT OF A FIVE-YEAR-OLD

"When my child started in the big-kids' room, the playing was very different. It was all yelling and wrestling and pushing and shoving."

—MIRIAM, PARENT OF A FIVE-YEAR-OLD

"It's a very difficult thing, with boys. We don't really know what to do when they're shoving each other really hard like that when they play. They're all included, and no one's crying, so I guess it's okay?"

—IDA, TEACHER

Boys are exposed to more violence than girls, and adults often see this violence taking place. When a group of boys are pushing and tackling each other until they fall down, or pile on to each other until someone starts crying, it often takes a long time for adults to do anything about it. What are we telling children when we let them carry on until someone starts crying? What would we do if it were a group of girls who were kicking each other? One important reason that boys are

exposed to more violence committed by other boys and that we think of it as natural is related to ideas about "manliness." Manliness entails being invincible and tough. Instead of the adults intervening, the behavior is explained as "boys being boys" or "they need to test their limits."

Why is it that so few girls test their limits in this way? If girls were to start knocking each other down or tackling each other roughly, there's a pretty good chance that adults would intervene and tell them to find something else to do. But when boys do it, many adults are uncertain whether it's okay to step in. *Is it really such a big deal?* they wonder while trying to remember what it was like when they were little. Boys fought back then, too, and nothing bad happened, right?

When we ignore playing that involves violence, we normalize violence precisely because we choose to see it as a game and not as violence. Meanwhile, the home, playground, and preschool are supposed to be safe and secure places for everyone. No one should have to be afraid of being hit or pushed. Imagine if we adults were shoved roughly when we arrive at work or kicked in the shins at lunch? Another big factor is that much of children's culture that targets boys, from movies to games, involves a lot of violence. In *Teenage Mutant Ninja Turtles* and *Star Wars*, the fight against evil takes a decidedly more brutal form than in *Bamse*, even if Bamse the bear is resorting to rougher and rougher tactics these days. Those narratives rarely focus on being kind or listening and respecting each other's limits.

In order for physical games to work, children need to know that there are still rules. And they need to be open to learning those rules and stopping what they're doing before they go too far. Instead of assuming that they'll learn where the limits are when they go too far, when someone has collapsed and is crying, we need to understand that certain games are tied to maturity. We don't let young kids drive and then start talking about where the limits are once they've crashed.

Suggestions

Organize wrestling games and play tug-of-war and other games where all children can test their physical strength in a safe environment, with an adult who will intervene before it's too late. That way, children can practice fine-tuning their own strength and understanding each other's feelings without it all going too far.

Always say something when children are fighting, even if they say they're just playing.

If you don't know what to say when children are play-fighting, fighting, or pushing each other, you can simply say:

- *Stop.*
- *Stop that.*
- *It's not okay for you to be fighting.*

You don't have to provide a long explanation about why it's not okay.

Every now and then, ask children if they've been pushed, kicked, or anything like that. Ask them how they felt when it happened. Introduce a zero-tolerance policy for behavior that can harm others. Explain to children why it's important not to harm anyone, even in a game. And teach them words they can use to stop what's happening if they end up in that situation.

Have children practice resisting. If someone pushes them, they don't have to push back. If someone says something mean, they don't have to say something mean back. But in order not to, they need strategies. Talk to children and prepare them for what they can do instead. For instance, they can say: *Stop it! I don't like it when you do that!* And then leave.

Teach children to fold their arms across their chests to help them stop themselves from hitting back.

Teach children to speak out if they see someone who is fighting. It's important to understand that you are part of what's happening if you are standing by and watching, even if you're not active. This offers an opportunity to talk with children about moral courage and why it's important.

As an adult, be clear about rejecting all forms of violence by always taking action in incidents that involve violence. This shows the child who's subjected to violence and the child who's perpetrating it that violence is not okay.

Soccer or Ballet

"We practice soccer together every day. He's developing an amazing shot."

—JOHN, PARENT OF A FOUR-YEAR-OLD

"I really hope Nillan wants to take up riding when she's a little older. Horses are so sweet. I love their large eyes and soft muzzles."

—PATRICIA, PARENT OF A THREE-YEAR-OLD

"My son was supposed to play in a basketball tournament in third grade. They had an energetic team, with both boys and girls. When they got to the tournament, the organizers refused to let a mixed team play. I was so angry—my blood was boiling, and I felt so stupid when I tried to explain to the children that they weren't allowed to play."

—MARIA, PARENT OF A NINE-YEAR-OLD

"I don't know what to do. Ivar doesn't really engage at his tennis lessons. He seems to mainly want to watch. Soccer, too."

—CLAES, PARENT OF A FIVE-YEAR-OLD

Sports and other after-school activities are about so much more than the actual activity. Every sport is its own microcosm of friends, competitions, camps, and other parents.

It's about social interactions and about learning codes, behaviors, norms, and values. And, just like everywhere else, everything is gendered. There are very clear ideas about which activities girls are supposed to like and which ones are for boys. Girls are encouraged to do gymnastics, to dance and sing, or ride horses, and boys are encouraged to play basketball, soccer, table tennis, and hockey. Many sports have teams divided by gender from a very early age, even though there are no physical differences among children by gender in terms of speed, strength, or flexibility when they're little. Children are sorted by gender as if it were the most natural thing in the world, so natural that we often don't even think about it. Children do not always choose their activities themselves. Often, their choices are made by whatever is locally available, what their parents want their kids to be good at, or what their parents wish they could have done, when they were young or even now.

Girl-soccer

Myths and values associated with different activities are strong. Many people think that girls who do horseback riding are mainly just cuddling with the horses. Girls riding horses are rarely conceived of in terms of the courage and strength that the riding requires. Dancing requires strength

In 2019, 28 members of the US women's national soccer team sued the United States Soccer Federation over unequal pay. From 2016 to 2018, the US women's team generated slightly more revenue than the men's team, but were paid less than half as much per game.

155

and knowing your body and having good coordination; playing soccer or hockey requires being receptive and able to work with others. Many sports have sexist features and widespread homophobia. Women's soccer is typically considered less exciting and just not as good as men's soccer, and traditional boys' sports rarely have room for sensitivity unless it's labeled "girly" or "wussy." Boys who dance are admired by girls but often considered unmanly by men.

Suggestions

What does your child enjoy doing? Choose recreational activities accordingly. Let your child try several different activities to have an idea of what's involved and be able to choose.

Ask instructors to highlight characteristics that are not typically noted in the various activities:

- *What strong muscles you must have since you're a dancer.*
- *You're so brave to ride a horse.*
- *You must be very good at teamwork since you play soccer.*
- *Wow, you must have an awesome sense of balance as a skater.*
- *I guess you know very many words since you read so much.*

If children are divided by gender at practice or into boys' teams and girls' teams, ask the coach what the reasoning is behind this and suggest that they all play together instead. Show your child role models who break gender stereotypes by choosing different activities and sports. Carolina Klüft, the track and field athlete, Marta Vieira da Silva, world champion soccer player, Diana Nyad, long-distance swimmer, Jonathan Groff, star of musicals, Rudolf Nureyev, the very skilled ballet dancer, Tina Thörner, world-famous rally car navigator.

Come Celebrate!

It's your child's birthday and they want to have a party and invite all their friends. You're going to have one kids' party and one party for family. Who should be invited? Should you invite the whole preschool class, or just certain children? When your child says that she only wants to invite the girls, you might think that's an easy way to solve the problem. She only ever plays with the girls anyway, so of course she wants to invite them.

Boy parties and girl parties are gender traps that we step into by letting gender be an acceptable category for segregating children and for excluding certain children. Few parents would put up with their children only wanting to invite blond or short children, or only the loud children or only funny children. Parties are often important events for children, and who gets invited can be a big deal, at least for young children. Children also signal not wanting to be friends with someone by saying: *You can't come to my party!* Not being invited is never fun, and it's even worse to be excluded based on your gender. Let's consider what we as adults are teaching children and what signals we're sending them when we approve segregated parties.

You can't come to my party!

Suggestions

If it's possible to invite all the children in a class, do it. The party could be an opportunity for the children to get to know each other in new ways. Parties don't have to be expensive: Being together in a large group and playing is all the fun that's needed. Throw a different kind of party. Meet up in the park and have a potluck, or meet at the public pool and invite the parents, too. Throw a monster party, pizza-making party, doctor party, or aerospace party so that all children can be included and try new roles. You'll create a sense of togetherness since everyone is trying the same thing.

Gender Equality in Friendships

When children interact with one another, they can try on new roles, characteristics, and skills. Gender equality in friendships has to do with seeing all children as potential friends. If we had gender equality in friendships, no children would be excluded because they had the "wrong" gender. No one would be blamed by default when an interaction isn't working out. Children would be able to take part in competing and collaborating. Choosing to be part of a group would be as natural to them as it would be to challenge the group. They would learn that conflicts can be solved and that it can be exciting to go your own way. Children would see differences as something positive and have more room to shape their own identities and friendships.

Big Boys Don't Cry

More Ways of Feeling

Dry Your Tears!

When really young boys cry, no one bats an eye; we comfort them the same way we comfort all young children. But as time goes by, boys' tears dry up. They learn that crying is not for them. Boys who cry are met with tired sighs and irritated looks. Or else they're told to buck up and cheer up. Something clearly happens to us when we encounter boys who are crying. But this wasn't always the case. Among the European nobility in the 1700s, "real" men were supposed to be able to show their emotions and cry. This is foreign to the contemporary ideal, which sees men's crying as a sign of weakness. Crying means losing con-

It's nothing!
Up you go!

You're such a big boy. You shouldn't be crying.

trol, and there are many men who've never cried despite facing very difficult challenges and personal tragedies. For men to cry at all, it has to take place in solitude with no one there to hold them or place a warm hand on their shoulders. Tears are for girls and women, clearly. Even if far from all women cry, the barrier to crying, whether alone or in public, is not at all as high as it is for men.

He's just a little sensitive.

Since we rarely see men cry, it's easy to get the idea that men and boys don't get sad. But that's as backward as the notion that their tear ducts are blocked. Instead, boys and men have simply been forced to shut down their feelings of sadness and transform them into feelings that are more accepted. It's hard to experience difficult emotions and not let the tears flow. Being sad often evokes a lot of other emotions, and we want everything to be alright again, which means many adults try to smooth things over. The ability to validate your own feelings and allow yourself to be sad and express sadness are necessary conditions for being healthy and developing self-awareness and empathy.

Suggestions

Let all children experience their tears and sad feelings, even if it feels hard. Don't smooth things over; stay close to them, hold them, and let their sadness take time so that you're demonstrating that it's okay to be sad.

Let boys, especially, cry and help them put words to their emotions. Tell them that tears are good because they help get the sadness out of the body so it doesn't have to stay there.

Movies and books can offer good role models for feelings. Talk about situations in which men and boys have cried when they've been sad.

Show your child that you cry when you're sad and that sadness is a feeling that exists and something that passes. Name your own emotions:

- *Now I'm sad.*
- *I'm crying now because I'm sad, but it will pass in a while.*
- *I'm feeling upset right now and need to be upset for a little while.*

Play games with your child where you imagine situations that are sad. Show that it's okay to cry and to comfort by exploring how to express sadness and how to comfort someone.

Sad Becomes Angry Becomes Sad

"My sister's such a crybaby. She cries over the smallest thing and runs to daddy and tells. But not my brother. He just gets up and keeps on going."

—MARCO, BIG BROTHER OF A THREE-YEAR-OLD AND A FIVE-YEAR-OLD

"He's angry and throws tantrums almost all the time. I don't know what it is or what to do. But I guess he's at that age now."

—STEFAN, PARENT OF A SIX-YEAR-OLD

Adults teach girls from
a very young age to
mask their anger so
that, after time, it is
even unrecognizable
to themselves.
—Sharon Lamb, *The
Secret Lives of Girls:
What Good Girls Really
Do—Sex Play, Aggression,
and Their Guilt,* 2001

"Girls cry so much. It's hard to take all the fake tears seriously."

—CHRISTEL, DAY CARE TEACHER

Since our culture gender-codes feelings so thoroughly, children learn to transform their feelings into the accepted and expected form early on. If we see two kids on the jungle gym, and one of them is crying and the other one screaming and kicking, we typically interpret the crying one as sad and the kicking one as angry. But it might be the exact opposite.

Boys are taught to transform sad feelings and express them as anger and frustration, which are much more accepted ways of expressing themselves than crying. For girls, it's the opposite: their anger is transformed into sad feelings and is expressed by crying. What happens is that two emotions are joined together and expressed as the same emotion. Eventually, it makes it difficult for children to distinguish between the two emotions. Both anger and sadness are important feelings. Anger signals where our limits are and allows for a forceful *no*. When we're sad, we're showing what's valuable and important to us.

Children who cry a lot may not have any other ways of expressing their feelings. Similarly, children who fight and fuss a lot may be using the only way they know how. They might be sad inside and might long for a warm hug, but instead they're met with cold words and pushed away. The more they fight

166

and fuss, the further from that warm hug they'll find themselves, and the more they'll continue to fight and fuss.

There's another aspect to difficult emotions. If children don't learn how to handle difficult emotions, there's a great risk that they'll hurt themselves or others. Girls often turn inward with their feelings, becoming quiet and critical of themselves, while boys act out and become troublemakers. How we deal with our emotions affects how we feel, both as children and later in life.

Suggestions

Help children tell the difference between being sad and being angry by validating and naming all of their feelings:
- *I see that you're angry.*
- *I see that you're sad.*
- *I see that you're frustrated.*

Hold children when they are sad *and* when they're angry. By being there to share their feelings, you're showing them that both emotions, sadness and anger, are okay.

What strategies do you have for dealing with your anger? Talk to your child about what you can do when you're angry. For instance, it might help to stamp your foot hard on the floor and

say very loudly, *I'm so angry!* Or maybe go outside and yell at the top of your voice.

Instead of saying, *You're not allowed to hit*, hold your child and say calmly, *We don't hit*. This lets you affirm the child's feelings but avoid shaming and blaming them. You also send the message that hitting is not okay even if you're angry.

Draw faces representing a variety of feelings. Your child can draw their own pictures of faces to express a feeling, or point to pictures of different faces expressing different emotions. The faces can be used in conflicts to name feelings.

We're all different. Explain that people feel happy, sad, frustrated, angry, and frightened about many different things. Because we're different, sometimes it's hard to understand each other's feelings, and that's why it's important that we talk with one another about how we're feeling.

Decisive or a Handful

"We're having some problems with our daughter."
"I see . . ."
"She's so stubborn."
"Okay . . ."
"Well, you know what happens to girls like that when they grow up.
*   They have a hard time. So, we need to do something."*

We want girls to claim their space, take what's theirs, and speak out. But just as with boys and crying, it's only okay up to a certain point. It's not quite as bad to be a stubborn girl who acts out as it is to be a boy who cries a lot, but almost Stubbornness in a boy is taken to be a sign of endurance and awareness and of being strong-willed, while stubborn girls are seen as tiresome and annoying and as having been raised poorly. The very same behavior is described in entirely different ways depending on the child's gender. The different words we use carry different values. It's much better to be strong-willed than to be tiresome, better to be stubborn than contrary. The words we use to interact with our children affect how they see themselves, and the extent to which they dare test, develop, and push their own thoughts and ideas.

Suggestions

Take stubbornness in all children as something positive that stems from a strong sense of purpose. Support all children's uniqueness by letting them put their own thoughts and ideas into practice. Let them come up with a recipe for the cake and bake it to see if it works. Let them walk barefoot in the rain to see what that feels like and whether they enjoy it. Let them try wearing their shirts as pants. Having an idea and carrying it out builds confidence and self-esteem.

Don't guilt children; instead, help them understand and name their own emotions. Validate their feelings by telling them how you usually react in a similar situation. That way, the focus shifts away from the child, which means they don't have to stay on the defensive.

I can tell that you are angry, and I see that you are hitting. When I'm angry I usually go outside and bang on a tree. Would you like to try that?

Role models are important. Talk about past and contemporary stubborn and inventive girls and women. Here are a few examples: Jane Goodall lived with and did research on gorillas. Anna Lindh was Sweden's foreign minister. Stephanie Kwolek invented the super-strong material called Kevlar that's used for trampolines and bulletproof vests. Amelia Earhart was the first woman to fly across the Atlantic, twice.

Now That's a Good Girl!

"Selma is such a good girl. She gets dressed on her own. I never have to help her."

—NICOLAS, PARENT OF A THREE-YEAR-OLD

"She plays so well. She's so good at adapting."

—KAREN, PARENT OF A FOUR-YEAR-OLD

"What a brave boy to have your blood drawn! Is your little brother as brave as you?"
"She's my little sister, not my brother, and I'm not a boy."
"Oh! What a good girl you are having your blood drawn, then."

—PEDIATRICIAN, TALKING TO A FIVE-YEAR-OLD

Being "good" means taking responsibility, helping, and performing well. That all sounds fine. But if we add that being good also means pleasing others, it's not quite as exciting. The word *good* is most often used for girls when they follow rules, do what they're told, and make things easier for others. They're also told that they're good when they draw,

You're good at drawing!

get dressed, have had a shot, or play with blocks. Many girls are constantly told that they are good no matter what activity they engage in. The goodness mantra starts at an early age for girls. Being good becomes a way of getting recognition and attention. But the crux is that good children easily come to forget themselves. A good girl is a child who is skilled at reading her environment's expectations and adapting to them. Her own desires and needs are set aside.

You're a good girl to climb so well!

If children are told that they are good no matter what activity they're doing, being good becomes part of their identity. They quickly learn that what they do for others is what's important, not who they are. When good girls no longer can live up to the others' expectations, they fail. Instead of questioning the reasonableness of what's required of them, they feel guilty and think there's something wrong with them. If they only try a little harder, make themselves look a little nicer, read what others want a little better, then maybe they can still be good girls. In the adult world, good-girlness takes its toll. Many women can't take being a wonderful wife,

You're such a good helper!

caring mother, passionate lover, inspiring friend, and awesome colleague or boss. Burnout and other symptoms of fatigue are not unusual among those who strive to live up to the ideal.

Suggestions

Recognize and name characteristics and activities, rather than your child's goodness:

- *How fun that you've baked a cake!*
- *How curious you are!*
- *How inventive you are!*
- *You get dressed very eagerly.*
- *You're so fun!*
- *You're careful when you build.*

Ask questions and give children a chance to describe their experiences themselves instead of telling them they're good.

- *How did you go about cleaning your room?*
- *How did you balance all the bowls when you carried them to the kitchen?*

Use the word good sparingly, especially with girls. They're already told in so many different ways that they're supposed to be good. Confirm what a child is doing without evaluating it. Confirmation and recognition can go quite far!

- *I see that you are climbing.*
- *I see that you are drawing.*
- *I see that you are parking the car.*

Teach all children to ask for help when they need it. Accepting help does not mean that you're weak or somehow less good as a person. Accepting help is brave, and it's something adults could practice doing.

That's Enough!

At the preschool Solrosen, the children are sitting in a ring. Lisa, Milla, and Eskil are talking with each other and are having a hard time sitting still. The teacher gives Lisa and Milla a stern look and says, *Get it together girls—it's circle time. That's enough!* As with stubbornness, the tolerance level is different depending on the gender of the child who's testing the limits and rules. Girls are expected to understand and follow rules better than boys. Which means that girls end up being more careful, on average, than boys about following rules. Girls often become the rule police. They try to control what gets done and by whom. Boys are indirectly encouraged to test and break rules, since nothing much happens when they do break existing rules. Rule violations are excused on account of boys having all that "boy energy," or "boys being boys," or it just being a "boyish prank." Instead of being reprimanded, boys are often seen as naturally creative, bold, and strong-willed when they don't adapt to the rules of the game. The crux here is that this backfires on boys in the long run. It becomes hard for them to tell when it's a good thing to over-step limits and when it's definitely not allowed. For girls, it's the opposite. The more important it is to get it right, the more energy they spend on correcting things, and the harder it is to paint outside the preexisting lines. All children need to learn which rules are absolute and which ones are negotiable. In life, we need to be able to identify and follow rules, as well as dare to question the rules that already have been established. To a large extent, creativity has to do with daring to turn things upside down to find new ways of thinking and doing.

Suggestions

"The hand" can be used as a method to teach children to wait their turn. Put your hand up as a stop sign for the person who interrupts. Do not make eye contact with the person who wants to interrupt. Finish talking. When you're done, turn to the interrupter and give them affirmation:

So great to see that you've waited your turn. What was it you wanted to say?

Before you introduce this method, talk it over with your child. Many children will in turn use the method for when they don't want to be interrupted by others.

Talk to children who don't follow rules, or often challenge them, about what the rules are good for and why they're important. Offer positive feedback and recognition when rules are being followed.

Make sure to show children who are very concerned about following the rules that rules aren't always absolute. Girls, especially, need to understand that sometimes there's room to modify instructions, rules, and limits, and that doing so can be positive.

It's better to establish a few rules and make sure that they're really adhered to, than it is to have a lot of rules that you don't have the time or energy to enforce.

Take responsibility for making sure that rules are followed and talk about the fact that you are doing this. That helps children not have to be the rule police at the expense of their own creativity.

Participate in games and play with your child, letting them decide on the rules. The journey may prove exciting and it's a wonderful thing for children to be in charge and get to set the rules instead of just following them.

In the US, three-quarters of sexual assaults are not reported to the police.
—US Bureau of Justice Statistics, National Crime Victimization Survey, 2010–2016 (2017)

A "No" of One's Own

"Joel, can you help me pick up the toys?"
"I'm building."
"Karin, perhaps you can help?"
"I'm building, too."
"Someone has to help me. It won't take long. Come on, Karin."
"But I didn't use them."
"No, but we've agreed that we all have to help, right?"

All children have the basic right to say both *yes* and *no* and to be heard. They have the right to express what they want and to signal where they draw the line. But *no* isn't always taken to mean no. Many people interpret a girl's *no* as negotiable. It might be a question of trying to persuade them to paint and draw since the materials are already set out, or it might be to make them do something they really don't want to do. A boy's *no* is seen as a sign of decisiveness, that he really knows what he wants, and is met with greater respect. Children quickly learn the rules of the game. When your *no* is not met with respect, you grow uncertain, you feel like you don't matter. Many children have no other recourse than running to get a grown-up, which earns them the label of "needy." Instead of reading their behavior as an expression of *no* not being respected, or that they can't make clear where they draw the line, they're seen as gossipy and whiny.

Every time they have to use an adult to get a result and have their voices heard, and every time we as adults assume the role of fixer, it grows harder for these children to find their own *no*. But how are children without a *no* of their own supposed to protest if they're the victim of verbal or physical abuse? We're only able to say *yes* or *no*, and own it, once we respect our own feelings.

Suggestions

Help all children develop their own clear *no*. Saying *No!* or *Stop!* with a loud voice and a hand held out as a stop sign works very well for young children, too. Teach your child to show where they draw the line. A good, simple method to practice is:

1. **Name what's happening:**	*You are teasing me.*
2. **Name your feeling:**	*When you tease me, I get sad.*
3. **Say what you want to have happen:**	*Stop teasing me.*

Follow your gut instinct! Sit on a swing with your child. Ask them how it feels in the pit of their stomach: Awesome, butterflies, or scary? Talk about how it's important to listen to your stomach and to trust your stomach. If it feels good in your stomach, it's a good thing: *Yes, it's an awesome feeling; I want to do this!* If it feels bad, that's a no: *No, it feels scary. I don't want to!*

Always ask a child if they want a hug before you hug them.

- *May I hug you?*
- *Would you like a hug?*

We have to teach all children about consent and the right to their own body. How do we know if someone wants to do something? Play together and tickle each other and talk about how you can see or know if the person who is getting tickled wants to be tickled.

Teach all children to ASK if they're not sure the other person really wants to do something. It's better to ask one time too many than to cross someone's limit. Once you start getting used to asking, it gets much easier!

- *Would you like me to tickle you?*
- *Would you like to wrestle with me?*
- *Would you like for us to hug each other?*

Teach all children to listen to each other when they say *no*. Practice by playing together. For example, let two children stand facing each other a couple of steps apart. Have one child approach the other one until the latter says *No*. The former then stops. Then the no-sayer can say *come* (yes) and then *no*, again. Talk about how it feels when someone hears and listens to the *no* and the *yes*.

Lovers' Quarrel

"Axel hit me today."
"What do you mean?"
"He hit me at recess."
"Why did he do that?"
"I don't know. The teachers said it's because he has a crush on me."

When boys hit girls or tease them, adults often say it's a sign of affection. Many people see it as a clumsy, clueless, and sometimes charming way of trying to interact. But if a boy hits another boy, few would try to smooth this over by saying that it's an expression of love and tenderness. A girl who hits a boy is not excused on account of love, either. Instead, she's told that hitting is not okay, and she's expected to take responsibility for her actions and to check in with the boy she hit. Hitting or being hit is never okay. Do adults believe boys are not capable of showing someone they like how they feel? Because it's crazily contrary to hit someone you like. Love is all about caring for someone and being close to them, not violence. What is it about us as adults that makes us so quickly and with zero thought accept the behaviors of certain boys instead of requiring that they express their feelings in a positive way? When someone pushes and teases to show that they like someone else, it's hard for them to get their message across. There's a fair chance that the behavior will have the opposite effect. And what would happen if the girls were to fight back?

Suggestions

Show all children, especially boys, how to express love in a positive way. Talk about how to tell someone you like them. Suggest that they write a note or maybe draw a picture.

Teach children to really check in—to make amends—instead of simply saying that they're sorry. Making amends can include blowing on a scrape, offering a hug, or finding a stuffed animal.

Talk about how violence is never okay, not even play-fighting.

If an adult or a child suggests that hitting or pushing are signs of affection, always speak up. Love has nothing to do with violence.

Will You Be My Valentine?

In 1973, the American Psychiatric Association removed homosexuality from its Diagnostic and Statistical Manual of Mental Disorders (DSM).

Illinois was the first US state to decriminalize homosexuality, in 1962; the US Supreme Court did not decriminalize homosexuality until 2003.

We've all heard about the princess who pines for the prince. The story includes a number of ideas about what love should look like. The prince is expected to be the active party, driving the action, while the princess is passive, waiting for the prince to come rescue her. The princess is also expected to want the prince when he finally comes to rescue her. She falls in love at first sight, delighted that someone wants her.

Our stories about love teach children how boys and girls are supposed to act in a relationship, and with whom they're supposed to fall in love. Boys are expected to fall in love with girls, and girls with boys. Girls are told that they can show that they're interested, but not too much, because the boys are expected to take the initiative. Pretty girls and tough boys are often highly esteemed, and girls and boys in stories often look a fair bit like Barbie and Batman. Our children are taught what they're supposed to look like and how they're supposed to act in order for anyone at all to fall in love with them. Wouldn't it be lovely to have a bit more variety and diversity in love stories? After all, all kinds of children can be shy, and all kinds of children can be full of initiative.

Suggestions

Talk about how girls can be in love with girls, with boys, and/or with children who don't identify as boys or girls. Similarly, boys can be in love with boys, girls, and/or children who don't identify as either boys or girls. And children who don't identify as either boys or girls can be in love with boys, girls, and/or children who don't identify as either boys or girls. We can be in love with many people, in many different ways.

Let the princess have all the prince's attributes and vice versa. Or create an entirely new story, with all new attributes for both princes and princesses: *Once upon a time, there was a prince who really wanted to get married. He sat at the top of his tower waiting for a suitor to show up. One day, he saw a cloud of dust on the horizon, stoking the hope in his heart! After a little while, he saw a horse. A princess had come riding on her beautiful, galloping horse. The prince and princess were married and lived happily together for the entire time their love lasted.*

Emotional Gender Equality

Having feelings and allowing ourselves to feel them and express them are important parts of our lives, both as children and adults. If we had emotional gender equality, all feelings would be allowed to exist: frustration, joy, indecision, and sadness—there would be room for all of them. The various feelings wouldn't be assessed as better or worse, and no child would have to renegotiate or adapt their feelings to fit other people's expectations. All tears would be taken equally seriously, and children would receive help to express their feelings in a way that doesn't hurt them, their bodies, or others. If we had emotional gender equality, all children would be equally heard when they say *no*, and all their limits would be respected. Emotional gender equality would mean the freedom to fall in love with whomever—concepts like straight and gay wouldn't exist. In love, there'd be no predetermined roles for who should do what and how.

Arms, Legs, *Snippor*, and *Snoppar*

More Ways for Bodies to Be

"My son has learned to make a lot of noise when he doesn't have his way. He uses his deepest voice. But it goes away when he hasn't been at preschool for a while—he'll use a much higher-pitched voice."

—MAGDALENA, PARENT OF A THREE-YEAR-OLD

"This is a man singing falsetto. He can sing with a woman's voice."

—COMMENTATOR ON RADIO SWEDEN

Woohoo Voice or Boohoo Voice

Adults will often use a different tone depending on whether they're speaking to a boy or a girl. Listen in on people speaking to babies, where the difference is often very pronounced. Girls are often spoken to with a bright and soft voice, while boys often get to hear the adult's normal speaking voice. The gendered tone is obvious in young children, too, where girls use a frailer and higher voice compared to boys. In children's shows and movies, the female characters have high-pitched, squeaky voices compared to the male characters who have deeper voices. Girls and boys quickly learn that there are boy voices and girl voices. Young girls are allowed to speak in a high pitch,

Speak louder! We can't hear you!

188

but some adults will correct a boy who uses a squeaky or high pitch, and tell him to "speak properly," the idea being that he should use a deeper voice.

Differences in how their voices are used and how they're allowed to practice using their voices have consequences for when and how they can express themselves. Those children who use a high-pitched and thin voice have a harder time making themselves heard than those who use a deeper and louder voice. Many boys have the advantage of getting to develop their vocal resources. They learn to speak from the belly because that's what's often required in order to use a deeper and louder voice. Having access to a strong voice lets them claim space and attention, both at school and, in the future, at work.

It's also easier to interrupt higher-pitched voices than deeper ones. At play, working on projects together in school, in debates and discussions, children with weak voices are often erased, not because their ideas are weak, but because these children can't make themselves heard in the same way. If you're interrupted over and over again, it's easy to think that your ideas aren't interesting, which makes you even more

Do you have to speak so loudly the whole time?

quiet. People who use high-pitched voices are often not taken as seriously as those who use lower pitches and are often not accommodated in the same way. Indirectly, we send the signal to boys that on account of their voices, they are allowed to take up more space. We send the opposite signal to girls: that they should speak less and take up less space.

Suggestions

Talk with your children about how voices can be used in different ways. Try a monster voice, a mouse voice, a whisper voice, and other voices. Tell them that different voices are good to use in different situations, and that they have different jobs. Show them a good voice to use when telling an exciting story, when sharing a secret, when calling for a friend on the other side of the playground, and when saying *Stop!*

Explain how using your belly when you speak is good for speaking loudly and powerfully. Try it out by placing a hand on the lower part your belly. When you use your belly voice, your belly will poke out when you speak. Practice by saying *sssssssssss* with force. Try saying *sss sss sss sss* in short bursts.

Take Your Seats, Please!

A woman sitting with her legs wide apart is often met with amused looks; it's not at all accepted in the same way it is for men. Men who instead sit with their legs close to each other or who sway their hips when they walk can also encounter raised eyebrows.

You throw like a girl!

Most of us aren't all that aware of our body language or how it might reinforce or moderate whatever we're saying verbally. When we're with children, our body language is as important as the words we choose and our tone of voice. Often adults use small movements when interacting with girls and more expansive movements when interacting with boys. In playing ball with children, this usually becomes extremely obvious. The ball is rolled or gingerly thrown at girls, as if girls wouldn't be able to catch it, or as if they might break if it hits them. By contrast, the ball is often bounced or thrown hard and high at boys. It's part of the fun if they have to run and jump to catch it. If a boy is hit by the ball, or if he falls, it's no big deal—it's just good practice for a future soccer career. Our body language reveals what we think about a child and a child's capacity to, for instance, catch balls. Expansive movements encourage children to take up a lot space, while small movements signal the opposite.

The body language we have access to affects our opportunities to take up space and speak, be heard, and to have things our way. Body language can help us communicate how we feel without necessarily naming the feelings. Gender-coded body language is a straitjacket that limits children's ways of expressing themselves.

In 2015, the Metropolitan Transit Authority of New York City added "Dude . . . Stop the Spread, Please" as a new slogan in its Courtesy Counts campaign.

Suggestions

Provide all children with physical challenges. Ball games, running games, dancing, and climbing. Feeling your body and knowing that it is strong and can do a lot of things helps build a good sense of self.

Supply children with a wide variety of body language expressions. Try it out together in front of the mirror to see what your faces and bodies look like when you're angry, sad, uncertain, surprised, determined, sneaky, scary, or amused.

When you're watching a movie or a show, mute the volume and try to interpret what the people are saying. Try to guess what's going on.

Challenge yourself to use your body in more varied ways when you're speaking. Stand with your legs far apart. Stand with them close together and see if there's a difference in what it feels like. Gesticulate with large motions and keep them close to your body. Try saying the same words using different kinds of body language to see if there's a difference.

Put on music and dance with small movements or large movements, jump high and low, jump far and spin around. This lets you discover the opportunities that can be found in your body.

Being Close

Boys often experience less physical intimacy than girls. This starts right away, when they're tiny babies. Baby boys get to soar like air planes and are spun around at some distance from our bodies, while girls get to stay in our laps. When they fall and get hurt or are sad, they're treated differently, too. Girls are held in our laps until their tears have dried, while boys often get a perfunctory hug and are encouraged to keep playing.

Eye contact is another way of being close. We look girls in the eye more often than we do boys. Many boys and men have a hard time looking people in the eye when they talk with them. Maybe this is because our eyes are the mirrors of our souls, and by looking someone in the eye, we let them see us. Avoiding eye contact helps us avoid getting personal. Looking someone in the eye is a signal of confidence, but it also means running the risk of revealing vulnerabilities.

The older children get, the more obvious it gets that access to intimacy and eye contact varies by gender. Boys are kept at ever greater lengths while girls continue to be held close by both friends and family.

Show all children warmth, holding them close, especially boys, and let them cry in your arms.

Seek eye contact with all children, especially boys, when you talk with them. Squat down so that you are level with them.

Play the blinking game and practice maintaining eye contact. Stand across from one another or stand in a circle if there are more than two of you. Agree on the rules:

One blink = say your name

Two blinks = start jumping

Three blinks = let's trade places

Soft or Rough?

Vilhelm is running around and yelling in the dining room. "Be quiet," says Annika. Vilhelm continues yelling. Annika walks up to Vilhelm and grabs his shoulder and shouts at him: "Be QUIET now!!"

How and when we touch children influences how they interpret physical contact. Whether the touch is positive or negative matters a lot. Positive touches—a soft pat on the head, or a kind hand resting on a shoulder—make our bodies release the hormone oxytocin. It makes us feel good and relaxed. Oxytocin makes us want to interact and promotes empathy. Positive physical contact is a building block in developing empathy! In general, girls receive more positive physical contact than boys, even though we know it's critically important for everyone. The older the boys get, the less positive touching they get. Boys are often touched in negative contexts, in conjunction with reprimands or conflicts. Negative touching is when someone grabs you, for instance your arm or your shoulder. Negative touching generates stress and aggression. It makes children put up their defenses against touching because they associate touching with something negative or scary. This association can persist in adulthood. Children who are exposed to negative touching indirectly learn that roughness solves conflicts.

Touching someone roughly or raising your voice escalates conflicts. Likewise, if we as adults demand eye contact in a difficult situation, it easily comes across as a show of power, where the one who is forced to look at the other has to yield, which easily makes things worse. In the long run, we end up teaching different genders different things about touching, which affects what kind of human touch they can offer others.

Suggestions

Touch all children in positive ways. A friendly hand on their shoulders or a soft nuzzling on their heads.

During a conflict, or a reprimand, try touching the child in a positive way instead of negatively. It can have a calming effect. When a small child pushes, shoves, or grabs someone roughly, show them how to touch softly and with kindness, instead.

Try using what's known as a low arousal approach in conflicts. Literally back up instead of grabbing the child. Sit down so that you are level with the child, instead of standing over them. Talk in a calm and quiet voice instead of getting angry and raising your voice. A quiet voice is calming and isn't threatening.

Don't require children to look at you in a conflict. Eye contact can be very uncomfortable when we're scared or don't trust a situation.

Boys Don't Sparkle

"My son is four and loves the movie Frozen *and wanted a shirt with sparkles and a scene from the movie on the front. He was so proud when he came downstairs at our relatives' house. When he reached the bottom of the steps, the adults started laughing and said, 'That's for girls.' He's never worn it again."*

—OMAR, PARENT OF A FOUR-YEAR-OLD

"My son loves sparkles and dresses, but he only wants to wear them at home. These days, he says those things are for girls. Secretly, he still loves them but only dares to wear them when no one is watching."

—SEYFI, PARENT OF A FIVE-YEAR-OLD

"That's a girls' shirt. I can show you the boys' shirts."

—CLERK AT LINDEX CLOTHING STORE

More and more boys want to wear sparkles and glitter. They aren't satisfied with the dark clothes in one section of the store. Just like girls, they want to be able to choose bright colors and dark jeans. And why not? Children, without knowing it, are challenging norms about masculinity, about how sparkles are feminine and shouldn't be worn by boys. When children happily pull on their sparkle shirts and head off to preschool, they might run headlong into that norm. Sometimes, being laughed at or hearing someone say, "That's a girls' shirt," can be as bad as being slapped, And it's easy to adapt and hide the favorite, special clothes way in the back of the closet.

Boys will often respond angrily, angry at the feminine instead of being angry at those who are being mean. They will denigrate or break things that are considered girly. For instance, a girl might wear a shirt they would like to have, but they'll call it ugly: *That's just garbage stuff for girls.* They'll make it sound like something bad, something worth less, while what's really going on is that they're angry because they are shut out from having access to what's considered feminine. Teaching boys to distance themselves from "the feminine" is part of the mechanism that keeps "femininity" subordinate to "masculinity."

It can be particularly painful when adults are mean, especially when it happens at preschool, which is supposed to be a place for children to try new things and develop free of limiting gender stereotypes. Many parents might keep the sparkles and glitter and other "feminine" accessories, like barrettes and nail polish, from boys to protect them from getting teased. But that's not a solution that strengthens their self-esteem. It's better to see children as strong individuals who are not satisfied with just the masculine and choose to support them so that they dare to meet and handle other people's reactions. For many years now, girls have been encouraged to stake a claim to everything that is coded as masculine, and to claim their right to the entire pie, not just half. Boys have that same right.

Suggestions

Let all children wear clothes with sparkles if they want to. Buy sparkly clothes online if you don't want to confront gender-segregated stores.

Children who challenge gender roles are strong people. Boys can handle some resistance when they want to approach things that are considered feminine.

If you feel you have to say something, try this: *Here you are, all sparkly!* to all children, irrespective of their gender. You don't have to say that they look nice; it's enough to simply recognize the sparkling.

Talk to any sales associates who tell boys that the clothes they choose are girls' clothes and vice versa. Try saying: *I know that you mean well, but my son likes sparkles.*

Be Careful!

"When the girls were climbing, they were told to be careful, and when they jumped down, they were told to sit down on their bottoms first and then jump down."

—RAIMO, PARENT OF A THREE-YEAR-OLD

"At gymnastics, the children were climbing on rope ladders. When girls were climbing, the instructors kept yelling at them to be careful. The instructors kept showing with their entire bodies that the children could fall any second. When boys were climbing, the instructors just stood there quietly."

—JOSEFIN, PARENT OF A FIVE-YEAR-OLD

Infants need a lot of care. They are almost completely helpless and can barely move. As they grow, so does their desire to explore the world. Starting out, they put everything in their mouths. Then they learn to sit up and to crawl. It may take a while, but eventually most babies learn that it's better to crawl feet first down the stairs. Children need a lot of space to learn to move around and practice their gross motor skills. Adults often have a hard time trusting that their children can manage things themselves, like feeding themselves or riding a bike. Our fear of them getting hurt will sometimes make us limit their development. The gender trap we can step into is

202

that most of us worry more about girls than we do about boys. Early on, girls have to learn to be careful and to look out. If children have to hear *Watch out! You could fall! Be careful!* over and over, that can put a damper on the joy of daring to test new things and being creative.

Suggestions

Instead of repeating *Watch out!* and *Be careful!* Tell children what they can do:

- *Ride on the smooth side of the road.*
- *Hold on to the large branch up there. That one is sturdy.*
- *Lie down flat on the ground so that the swing won't hit your head.*

Let all children try doing things on their own. Helping them or doing it yourself might be simpler and save time in the short run, but, in the long run, you're not doing your child—or yourself—any favors by not letting them do it themselves.

Catching yourself when you fall is a great thing to practice while playing. Practice on soft pillows or a soft carpet. Roll around and do somersaults and move around in ways that teach children to feel the possibilities of their bodies.

Play balance games in the woods, at the playground, or in other fun areas. Demonstrate that it's easier to keep your balance if you hold out your arms or crouch down a bit to steady yourself.

203

A child's cries don't always mean that they want to be picked up and cuddled. If you think everything is more or less alright, show the child that you are paying attention and ask questions. Sometimes children want affirmation and are more interested in showing how and where they got hurt than in being hugged:

- *I can see that you fell.*
- *You really caught yourself when you fell.*
- *Where does it hurt?*
- *What can you try to do to avoid falling?*

Strong, Thinner, Loveliest

"One of my friends gave my son a Batman costume. The costume was padded with large 'muscles.' I just have to wonder, though, if anyone would've thought it was okay to give a little girl a princess dress with fake breasts?"

—JOHAN, PARENT OF A TWO-YEAR-OLD AND A FOUR-YEAR-OLD

"My daughter complains about being fat almost every single day. It makes me so sad, and I just don't know what to do. She's so pretty and just six years old."

—FREDERICO, PARENT OF A SIX-YEAR-OLD

"My son got a cut above his eyebrow. When we went to the ER to get stitches, the doctor said he would have a cool scar on his forehead. Everyone we ran into said the same thing, that the scar was cool."

—SARAH, PARENT OF A FIVE-YEAR-OLD

"My friend's children were bitten by a dog when they were tiny— the girl, on her shoulder, and the boy, on his face. It was horrible, but the first thought that struck me was that it was a good thing it wasn't the girl who had been bitten on the face. These ideas we have about girls and beauty run deep."

—DIANA, PARENT OF A THIRTEEN-YEAR-OLD AND A FIFTEEN-YEAR-OLD

Boys who are strong and muscular and girls who are slim and pretty. Sound familiar? We see them every day in ads and commercials. Boys in briefs with six-pack abs or skinny girls in tight clothes. These images affect us, and instead of getting angry at them for not representing reality, we get angry at ourselves for not living up to them. Muscles are good because they make the body healthy, in much the same way that obesity is not good because it can lead to disease. But a wide range of possible appearances can be found between these two extremes. Marketers claim that everyone ought to understand that of course the images are airbrushed and

Approximately 20 million females and 10 million males in the US have a clinically significant eating disorder at some point in their lifetime.
—The National Eating Disorders Association

In 2016, Mattel introduced Barbies with curvy, tall, and petite body types.

altered and that they aren't real. But have we really kept up with the fact that hardcore photoshopping is standard practice these days? How are our children supposed to understand any of this?

Very few people can live up to the ideal and the stereotype. A lot of boys and girls spend hours on end at the gym or in the weight room building muscles, or burning fat and losing weight. Not all boys are big and strong, and not all girls are slim. Very few of them look like the pictures in the ads and fashion magazines.

For girls, the range of accepted body shapes is more limited than for boys. Those who don't fit inside that range have a harder time developing a strong sense of self-esteem and the feeling that they are fine the way they are. In society, the ideal image of a boy is of someone who's muscular, but this is not as strong a requirement as the one that says girls have to be slim. Once again, we step into the gender trap that tells girls that their worth is tightly tied to their bodies and how they look. At an early age, many girls find themselves gazing critically at their bodies in front of the mirror. It's sad for average-weight five-year-olds to complain about being fat. Boys are often free to be slim, lanky, or chubby; they're taught that their appearance isn't as big a part of their identity. To be sure, this is changing, and, more and more, boys are being drawn into this anxiety over appearances. They're supposed to be muscular and live up to the existing ideal for men. Boys are supposed to care about how they look, but not too much. A boy who lingers in front of the mirror is likely to be called "vain" or "girly." And neither label is meant as a compliment.

I don't think my dieting affects my children.

Suggestions

Encourage all children by focusing on characteristics that don't have to do with how they look. Talk about what they do, feel, and think, instead of how they look. This helps children develop a good sense of self.

Talk about how images in magazines and in ads aren't real, in the same way you explain that scary movies are made in studios—that it's make-believe.

Make sure children have access to magazines that aren't all about looks and bodies.

Talk about your own body with your child. What do you like about your body? By showing that you like yourself even though you don't look like the ideal, you help your child understand that those ideals aren't real or important.

Show your children how easy it is to manipulate images with an app or on a computer. Talk about how images are changed in order to catch people's attention and make us buy things.

But Her Hair Was So Pretty . . .

"Everyone thought Lukas was a girl when he had long hair. It got to be such a pain that I finally just cut it all off."

—ANNA, PARENT OF A THREE-YEAR-OLD

"I cut my daughter's long hair this past summer. Wow, did that ever bother people! We were constantly told it was a shame, that her hair had been so beautiful. And then they tried to make things better by saying that it would grow out again. Some of them came right out and said that girls are prettier with long hair."

—GUSTAV, PARENT OF A TWO-YEAR-OLD

"My niece hardly has any hair at all, but her parents insist on styling it with bobby pins and rubber bands."

—AMIR, UNCLE OF A TWO-YEAR-OLD

When they're very young, boys are allowed to have long hair. But once they're a few years old, out come the scissors. We might wish that boys and girls could get to choose for themselves how they wear their hair, but it's not always easy to break the unwritten hair rules. Being different and choosing your own path often means that other people want to try to correct you or comment on what you're doing. Most children "know" that girls have long hair and boys have short hair. Hair is strongly gendered and thereby fraught with meaning. Luscious, long locks spell *feminine* and short hair spells *masculine*. In general, very few girls have short hair. Girls very rarely have the same kind of crew cuts that many boys have. Short hair doesn't lend itself to barrettes and pony tails, but then again, no combs are needed to sort out tangles, either. Many parents are concerned about hair styles, worried that a style will turn out wrong, and their concern is rarely focused on anything practical. If it were, all kids would have short hair in the summer, and they would let it grow in the winter. For many girls, hair length signifies status within a group. The girl with the longest hair is the winner. Children are expected to follow gendered hair rules, and a girl who cuts off her long hair and a boy who won't cut his can count on having their choices questioned.

Suggestions

Tell all children that their hair is nice, whether it's short or long.

Let children try having long hair and short hair, so that they can see what it feels like and what they prefer. Short hair can feel good in the heat, and it doesn't get in the way when you're playing. Long hair is warmer and can cover your ears and keep them warm and can be fun to hide behind or style into pony tails and braids.

Include wigs as part of options for playing dress up. It's fun for all children to have a chance to see what it feels like to have different hairstyles.

If a child changes their hairstyle, comment on the fact that a change has occurred, rather than on how they look:

- *I can see more of your face now. That's fun!*
- *What does it feel like when you shake your head?*
- *Did you get to hold the scissors yourself?*

What Do You Have Between Your Legs?

The word *snopp* (penis, willy; pl. *snoppar*) entered the Swedish language in the 1960s. In 2006, the word *snippa* (vulva and vagina; pl. *snippor*) was included in the dictionary of the Swedish Academy.

"My brother is so proud that his son has 'found his thing, already!' I've never heard a parent say the equivalent about their daughters when they've found their 'things.'"

—MIA, PARENT OF A ONE-YEAR-OLD

Girls rarely get to experience the pride with which boys talk about their penises. Instead, they are taught to keep quiet about what they have between their legs. Obviously, this will affect how they think about their genitals, their bodies, and their worth. Boys' views of girls are affected, too, since, it's easy for them to come to the conclusion that girls are lacking something. Which, of course, is completely wrong: girls have their *snippa*. In English, we still don't have accurate terms in standard use for a girl's genitals.

Some people feel that it's culturally insensitive to talk about vulvas and vaginas. Sure. In most cultures, including Swedish culture, the reigning gender inequality dictates that women's genitals be rendered invisible. But all children, irrespective of their origins, need access to positive words that describe their bodies. Only then can we talk about vulvas and penises in the same matter-of-fact way that we talk about other body parts, like ears and feet.

The point is to name all body parts so that we can talk about the body and how it works.

Don't forget to wipe your snippa!

Suggestions

Start using the words *vulva* and *vagina* if you don't already and notice how proud girls are to have words for their genitals. As an adult, you will also appreciate having a word for "down there." Or why not try the Swedish *snippa*?

Family nicknames for body parts are also fine. Nicknames can show that a body part is important, one to be proud of.

Use accurate terminology for your own genitals when you talk with children. It's easier to communicate when you use the same terminology for adults and children.

If it's hard for your daughter to see her vulva, give her a "*snippa* mirror," so that she can see it all, including the labia and her clitoris. It's easier for boys to see their scrotum and penis.

Who Can Touch?

Throughout history, children have played games in which they explore their bodies. But adults have had different limits for what's okay for vulvas and vaginas and for penises. In Sweden in the seventies, we took for granted that children might find it pleasurable to touch their genitals. Today, many adults have a hard time talking about the fact that children might enjoy touching themselves. Is this because we're embarrassed, or are we worried children will injure themselves when they explore their bodies? It seems especially hard for adults to accept that girls touch their genitals. Boys tugging at their penises somehow seems more natural. Perhaps this is because it dangles loose and is easy to grab onto, but it probably has more to do with history and conceptions of male and female sexuality.

If we don't talk with children about their vulvas and penises in a positive light, as parts of their bodies that it can feel good for them to touch, we risk shaming them and guilting them about their bodies. What are they supposed to think when they realize it feels good but that it's not allowed? When we don't name what they do, we leave them vulnerable to society's stereotypes about female and male sexuality. Narratives about youth sexuality and adult sexuality are not gender equal.

Boys and men are described as having strong sexual urges. Girls and women can be interested in sex, but they're rarely described as having sexual needs. Women who have many sex partners will often be called "whores" or "sluts," which are not flattering terms. Men with many sex partners are admired and called "players" and "studs." The exact same behavior is considered positive for boys and negative for girls.

Suggestions

If a child is playing with their genitals, validate their behavior and explain that it's okay to explore your own body:

- *I notice that you're touching your snippa/snopp.*
- *I notice that you're exploring your body, but we're eating right now, so you'll have to do that later.*
- *I notice that you're touching your vulva/penis. Everyone does that from time to time.*

Try to provide straightforward answers to questions about genitals and sexuality. Children take in a lot that leads to questions, and simple answers are better than none. Young children are not embarrassed about bodies. They are curious.

Don't saddle children with adult ideas about sexuality. Validate them in their discoveries—that's all they need.

Explain that their genitals are theirs and that they decide whether to touch them and how. Just like children get to decide whether or not they want to fiddle in their nose. By giving children a chance to explore what feels good, you give them the context they need, should something at one point not feel good.

Talk to Adriana and Gustav about their bodies, about the vulva and penis. This will provide the basis for a positive and responsible sexuality, and they'll benefit from that their entire lives.

Real Boys Stand Up

"Mattias could already stand up and pee when he was two. He had to stand on a step stool in order to reach. He was so proud."

—JOHN, PARENT OF A FOUR-YEAR-OLD

"At our child's preschool, there are unofficial girls' bathrooms and boys' bathrooms. Many children, mainly girls, avoid certain bathrooms since there's usually pee on the seat or around the toilet. But how much fun is that for a boy who wants to sit down, or for anyone who needs to poop? For children, this is their work environment."

—JOSÉ, PARENT OF A FOUR-YEAR-OLD AND A FIVE-YEAR-OLD

"It's not okay to require that my child sit down to pee. He should get to pee standing up."

—MALIN, PARENT OF A FOUR-YEAR-OLD

Mom, why do grown-ups think boys are always gross when they go to the bathroom?

When children leave diapers behind and start using a potty, they take joy in observing what they've produced. At that very moment, no one thinks that boys and girls should behave in different ways. All children sit on potties. After some time, boys start standing up to pee in toilets. The question

218

of whether boys should stand up or sit down when they pee might seem inconsequential, but it often provokes strong emotions. Why? And why do many prefer to have even young boys stand up to pee? Because it's simpler and more convenient for boys, or because it shows that they will develop into men?

Look, I'm going to sit down to pee!

The public spaces we depend on are often designed not to meet our needs but to reflect old traditions and ideas. How else can we explain that boys have urinals while girls have stalls with locks? We don't question the idea that men can and want to stand next to each other to pee. But far from all men are comfortable with urinals for the simple reason that they're not comfortable showing their genitals or seeing those of others. Girls don't have to publicly announce whether they're peeing or pooping, while boys do, since you can't do the latter in a urinal. In many countries, there are urinals where both women and men can sit or stand as they see fit, and plenty of girls enjoy the simplicity of peeing quickly in a urinal. Furthermore, for trans people, the gendered bathrooms that exist in some public spaces can complicate going to the bathroom.

Suggestions

Encourage all children to sit down to pee while they still have a hard time aiming. This makes things more pleasant all around.

Pay attention to whether the boys' bathroom is not as clean and nice as the girls' bathroom. Having a nice and clean space is important for all children.

Suggest that the preschool or school provide a gender-neutral bathrooms. Most children are used to gender-neutral bathrooms from home.

In warm weather, all children can stand up to pee outside. You can teach girls to separate their labia and stand with their legs apart in the same way you teach boys to hold on to their penises to avoid spraying pee all around.

Nice Girls Don't Fart

"When we had a snack at our neighbors' house, their daughter spilled ice cream on her shirt. It was just a tiny spot, but her parents joked about how they were going to have to put her in the washing machine along with all her clothes. Their son was sitting next to her with banana all over his shirt and no one said a word about it."

—CHRISTIAN, PARENT OF A THREE-YEAR-OLD

"I want my daughter to be nice and clean. She's not allowed to eat with her fingers, and I'd like for her to wear a bib. Stained clothes are such a drag."

—PATRICIA, PARENT OF A THREE-YEAR-OLD

"When my daughter farts, she'll happily ask, 'Was that you, Mommy?' Then she'll proudly pronounce that she was the one who farted."

—CARRO, PARENT OF A THREE-YEAR-OLD

Girls are often expected to stay cleaner than boys, both in terms of their bodies and their clothes. This plays out in the colors of their clothes: girls' clothing is often made in lighter shades than boys'. There's also a common conception of girls as being more interested in staying neat and tidy. They're supposed to like washing and combing their hair and changing their clothes when they get dirty. When boys get dirty, that's interpreted as them having a good time playing. It's amusing to be able to read off an entire day's worth of meals on their shirts. *He's in such a rush and talks so much that most of the food lands on his shirt.*

Girls get scolded sooner than boys when they pick their noses, burp, or fart. Nice girls aren't supposed to do that kind of thing. Boys can fart and burp together and laugh out loud. It doesn't matter whether they're 3, 13, 23, or 43 years old. Bodily functions are apparently much more natural among boys. Boys don't regularly place toilet paper in the toilet to mask the sound of what they're doing. Girls are taught that some bodily functions should be muted. Surely, it's not possible to be both a fancy princess and a loud farter? This might seem amusing, but it can have serious consequences. On average, one to two quarts of gas pass through the adult body every 24 hours. Without a safety valve, we get bloated and our bellies ache.

Suggestions

Don't be so fussy about keeping children, especially girls, clean. Let them play. Dress them in clothes that are practical and easy to wash.

Bodily functions are natural to all children. Explain that all people need to fart, burp, and poop. Fancy princesses, queens, and famous movie stars do it several times per day.

Try to maintain a relaxed attitude to bodies and their functions. Explain that holding it in can be good in certain situations but that it's not a good idea to do it often.

The Fastest One Wins

"One day, one of the boys didn't want to sit next to one of the teachers any longer. After several weeks, we found out why: He was scared. He'd heard that the teacher had a baby in her belly, and he was worried she was going to eat him, too."

—LENA, TEACHER

When we talk about where babies come from, we often tell the story about the egg and the sperm. We describe how the sperm swims fast to the egg, which sits there waiting. The fastest sperm wins. When we explain how sperm get to the egg, we often say that the penis is inserted into the vagina. These stories repeat a number of myths about male and female behavior. Couldn't we just as well say that the vagina takes hold of the penis? Or that the egg runs to the fallopian tube and decides which sperm can enter? Or that the egg and the sperm work together? Today, babies are made in many different ways, which means that there are many different stories about how babies are made, from insemination to in vitro fertilization. Similarly, love and families can take many shapes. Some children have a dad or a mom, while some have two moms. Some have a mom and a dad,

Stjärnfamilj (star family) = A family that consists of one or more adults and children. The term *star family* covers all family constellations and emphasizes love, care, and respect as the basis for a family, rather than biological ties. The term was coined in 2009. In Swedish, *stjärnfamilj* is pronounced almost exactly the same as *kärnfamilj*, nuclear family.

while some have two dads. Even though many children live in a family that is not a mother-father-child family, many people continue to speak as if the nuclear family is the correct format. This results in many children feeling excluded, their families made invisible.

Suggestions

Try telling the story about where babies come from as if it were any other story: There is a room behind the vulva and vagina inside the body, called the uterus. That's a space where a baby can grow. To make a baby, you need a sperm and an egg. The eggs are in the ovaries and the sperm are in the testicles. The eggs and the sperm have to mix to make a baby. The mixing can take place inside the body (through insemination or intercourse) or outside (in vitro fertilization). Then the egg gets to grow in the uterus for nine months. That's when the baby is ready and gets to come out. The baby comes out through the vagina, which is a very strong muscle that opens into the vulva. Sometimes an opening is made through the belly into the uterus (C-section) to take out the baby that way.

Explain that families come in many shapes and sizes. There are families with one parent, adoptive families, nuclear families, large families, and new families. Explain that all families are love-families and configured just fine the way they are.

How fast can the eggs run?

225

Bodily Gender Equality

How children feel about their own bodies affects their self-esteem and their developing identities. If we can help children of all genders see their bodies as something positive that can be used for all kinds of activities, then we will have given them a lot. If we had bodily gender equality, children would not be judged by their bodies, and their self-esteem wouldn't be embodied in their hair or their muscles. There would be room for everyone, whether they're known as her, them, or him. Bodies would be allowed to be functional, not reduced to something nice to look at. All children would have the opportunity to both claim space and make room, to practice fine and gross motor skills. Children could be proud of their genitals and know that they alone control their bodies, *snippor*, and *snoppar*. Bodily gender equality would also let children develop a strong sense of integrity and take a responsible approach to sexuality, with respect for themselves and others.

In Preschool

The Preschool Gender Equality Mission

sleep
11-12
hours per day

preschool 6-8
hours per day

home 4-6
hours per day

Most children spend more of their waking hours at day care or preschool than with their parents. After a few years at day care or preschool, children will have spent a full year's worth of hours there. That's the equivalent of three thousand kids' parties or fifteen thousand dinners. Children take shape during all these hours. They develop their identities and discover who they are. They develop language, learn to interact with others, get to know the range of their own emotions, and develop characteristics and abilities. They're also taught to be boys or girls.

Even if it's not always possible to choose an early education program for a child, it is possible to influence how it operates. Asking questions is a good start. Many teachers spend a lot of time and effort creating a safe and nurturing environment for children, and they appreciate parents who take an interest. It can also feel very good to know how the teachers work and what values they have. How do they interact with a sad child? How do they act when there's a conflict? How do they work to let all children develop a strong sense of self and feel safe? How do they ensure that children practice their gross and fine motor skills? What do they do to let children practice both speaking and listening, asserting themselves and waiting their turn?

In 1998, the preschool system in Sweden changed from being a day care system to being part of the overall educational system. All children in Sweden have the right to attend public preschool starting at age one. The preschool system has its own official curriculum, which, according to the Swedish Education Act, has to be designed in accordance with gender equality. In turn, the official curriculum requires gender equality to be integrated in all preschool activities—everything from how children are treated to the choice of activities and materials. Gender equality is part of the Swedish preschool value system, and preschools are required to organize their activities so that children mix, play, and learn together, irrespective of gender. Both the preschool curriculum and the Education Act are legally binding on everyone who works at a Swedish preschool.

Sweden's Discrimination Act, in effect since 2009, also governs how preschools and schools are run. It protects everyone, including the children, against discrimination. The Discrimination Act requires each individual school and preschool to have an action plan against abusive treatment that shows the measures the school is taking to promote the equal treatment of all children. According to the law, equal treatment means that all children irrespective of their "sex, transgender identity or expression, ethnicity, religion or other belief, disability, sexual orientation and age" have the right to be responded to as individuals and equally.

What Should Be Included in an Action Plan Against Abusive Treatment?

A vision that describes how the preschool staff pictures an equal preschool—including gender equality. The vision should apply to children as individuals and as a group.

An account and analysis of current activities in terms of gender, ethnicity, disabilities, sexuality, and religion. The account should be based on observations of the activities, and children and parents should participate. Observations can include how the teachers treat the children, how children choose what to play with, which children play together, what activities the children participate in, and what the general mood is among the children as a group.

Equality represents the equal opportunities and rights of all persons, irrespective of gender identity, ethnicity, religion, disability, sexual orientation, or age. Gender equality is part of the equality concept.

Goals that are concrete and that show *what* should be done, *how* it should be done, and *who* will do what. It's important for the goals to be for a certain timeframe and for there to be a schedule for implementation. If the goal is to provide a more diverse range of role models, one method could include reviewing the preschool's literature and assortment of toys and other materials from a gender perspective to ensure that these match the preschool's mission to promote gender equality.

Follow-up and assessment that examines whether the preschool has reached the goals and also provides information on methods that have worked and those that need further development. The same methods used for the account can be used for the follow-up to simplify comparisons and make changes easy to see.

An emergency plan that describes the actions teachers and administrators should take if a child or a parent experiences abuse. The emergency plan should also describe how to follow up on the event and how to communicate with those involved.

A plan for the continued development of expertise that describes the expertise among the group of teachers on gender equality and equal treatment, and what expertise needs to be developed going forward. This can include lectures, field trips to other pre-schools, literature, and staff exchange programs.

Children and parents should participate in the work on gender equality and equal treatment. This can happen through surveys, interviews, and individual conferences. Letting parents and teachers participate in creating the preschool vision for gender equality and equal treatment and against abusive treatment is a good idea. Parents can for instance discuss this and summarize their ideas at a parent conference.

The action plan against abusive treatment should be followed up, assessed, and revised at least once per year.

Questions from Preschool Teachers

"Many parents want their girls to look like little princesses. It's very hard to talk with them about this because they take it so personally."

—BERIT, TEACHER

"Sometimes when a boy arrives and there are only girls outside playing, his parents will ask us where the children are. They want us to go inside and bring out boys so that their child can stay outside and play. I just don't know what to say."

—GABRIELLA, TEACHER

"When we bring up gender equality at parent-teacher conferences, there's often no response. Parents prefer to hear about how we teach children counting and writing. It's as if they think 'that other stuff' has no bearing on their children."

—ADAM, TEACHER

Implementing gender equality in schools requires skills, curiosity, courage, and persistence. Here are some common questions teachers may have about working with parents who may not share their values, along with suggestions for how to think and talk about those values.

Teacher: What can we say to a parent whose child is rarely dressed for playing?

Clothing can be a sensitive and loaded issue because how we dress shows who we are and who we want to be. Address this issue at an early stage, during the transition period when a child first starts at the preschool. Explain that certain clothing can make it hard for children to participate in school activities. It can be useful to also mention that clothes and accessories easily become status symbols that exclude certain children. Explain that you do not acknowledge children on the basis of how they look or what they are wearing, but rather on the basis of their personhood because you want to strengthen their self-esteem. That way, parents don't have to be sad that their children aren't receiving compliments for how they look. They can rest assured that you see their children no matter how they dress. Together, parents and teachers can agree on clothes that are practical for preschool.

For parents: What are your thoughts about your child and their clothes? Just like adults, children want to look nice and get dressed up every now and then, but children want to and need to be able to play without being limited by their clothes. Teachers are not supposed to, and they can't, tailor activities around fancy clothing; children who have to be careful with their clothes are saddled with a huge responsibility. For more on this, see the gender trap "Dressing to Play or Dressing to Please" (page 66).

(page 66).

Teacher: One of the parents doesn't want their son to play dress up with dresses or play with dolls. How should we respond to this?

Explain that the preschool strives to let all children develop and practice a wide range of skills and roles. You can highlight the positive characteristics that playing with dolls can foster. The child has the opportunity to practice empathy and intimacy. Explain that dresses are considered an item of clothing that all children should have access to. The drama around dresses can be reduced with various activities, like dances, where all children wear skirts and dresses and dance together. Explain to children that becoming a good dancer requires a lot of strength and coordination.

For parents: What are you afraid will happen if your child plays with dolls or wears dresses? Many fathers care for their children these days, so it's natural for your child to want to try that role. Wearing a dress can be a way of feeling fancy or trying a new role. It's good for children's development and makes them more well rounded. We often transfer our own fears to children completely unnecessarily, and this becomes a burden for children. This is why it's important for parents to gain perspective on their own fears. Read more about this in the gender trap "He Gets to Be a Little Bit Different" (page 76).

Read more about this in the gender trap "He Gets to Be a Little Bit Different" (page 76).

Teacher: We really try to encourage boys to express intimacy and emotions. But it can feel pretty hopeless. They just walk away or are quiet.

If children aren't used to talking about or showing their feelings, it can be difficult to get them to do that. Showing your emotions means making yourself vulnerable, and that requires courage. Role play with stuffed animals and other figures who are sad, scared, or angry can be a good way to approach emotions. This lets children have a concrete example to talk about, and they don't have to get personal if they don't want to. Another option for responding to a child and helping them put words to their feelings is to draw faces that are angry, sad, or frustrated. Children can point to the face that matches how they feel. Getting children to feel safe and comfortable talking about their emotions is easier if you can share your own experiences. Talk about what makes you sad or scared and what you usually do when you feel like that. Talk about feelings on many different occasions so that it becomes a regular part of life.

For parents: It's often easier to be happy than angry or sad, but it's important not to judge emotions as better or worse. Talk about how emotions have to be allowed to exist even if they're difficult to deal with. Also explain that it's important to do something about these feelings, because otherwise they'll remain in your body. Talking about feelings provides a good opportunity to show that people are different and that different things make them sad, angry, and happy. For more on this, see the gender traps "Dry Your Tears!" (page 162) and "Sad Becomes Angry Becomes Sad" (page 165).

Teacher: When the girls play on their own, everything's fine. But as soon as Gabriel wants to join in, it all falls apart. How can we talk with his parents about this?

Boys generally receive more negative attention than girls and are often blamed when problems arise. It's important to offer boys positive roles that let them be helpful. Games are often governed by invisible rules that make it hard for new children to join in. Make the rules visible by observing how the children are acting, and talk with the children and your colleagues about these observations. Children who often play together develop common rules; it can be a good idea to create opportunities for children who rarely or never play together to do so. Try joining in and helping Gabriel join and find a positive role. Explain to the child's parents that their child sometimes has a hard time joining other children in playing but that you are working on it.

For parents: Talk to the teachers if you feel that your child is seen as the one who is often disruptive. Explain that you want all the children to have a chance to take part and try different games. Ask how you can work together to make things easier for your child. See the gender traps "It Was His Fault!" (page 131) and "I'm Not Welcome" (page 145) for more details.

Teacher: When we have an open house for new parents, they often ask how many girls and boys there are in the group. What should I say?

Many parents are worried that their child won't have any friends if there are few children of the same gender, or none at all. The idea that boys are supposed to play with boys and girls with girls is very common. Explain that you see the children as children and that you actively work to build relationships among the children so that everyone can be friends with everyone. No one is excluded based on their gender. Provide clear examples of how you do this. Explain that what you teach informs how you organize groups of children. In Sweden, if you were to create groups based on the number of boys and girls, or had separate groups for boys and girls without a specific pedagogical purpose, that would be an act of discrimination according to the Discrimination Act. Help parents recognize the measures you take to promote gender equality by collecting articles, books, and other materials pertaining

238

to gender equality on a shelf or a bulletin board. Write down what you are working on at any given time. This lets parents take part and lets them understand how the school operates.

For parents: Why is it important for you to know how many boys and girls there are in a preschool? Do you think there's a certain composition that's preferable? What are you signaling as a parent when you ask that kind of question? Read more in the gender trap "Oh, They're So Cute!" (page 129).

Teacher: I find it hard to verbalize what children gain from gender equality measures.

The preschool atmosphere becomes more accepting when gender equality is promoted. When children and adults don't have to spend as much energy on correcting their own and others' behavior in order to fit within the gender frame, there's more space for creativity. Feeling safe in the knowledge that you are seen and accepted frees up a lot of energy for curiosity. Differences and diversity become positive aspects. More children can begin to express their preferences, can claim their space, and can understand how conflicts can be resolved democratically. Starting out, there may be more chaos as 15 kids—rather than maybe just three—claim space and respect, but over time a more accepting environment is created for all children. Gender equality efforts at preschool generally make both staff and children have a better time at school. Fundamentally, this is about the work environment for children and their opportunities to develop as individuals.

Questions from Parents

Just like there are parents who don't share the preschool system's values, there are teachers who think girls should be girls and boys should be boys. They turn a blind eye to what the gender inequalities mean for children. This can be very hard for parents who want their children to be treated as individuals, not as a gender. Below, we've gathered questions from parents and offer suggestions for how parents and teachers can talk about these issues.

"The situations that arise at preschool are hard for me to handle. How can I make clear that I want Rasmus to be treated as an individual, not as a representative of his gender?"

—SANNA, PARENT OF A TWO-YEAR-OLD

"After a while, it became clear that my daughter was indeed drawing at preschool and making things, but the staff was giving all of that directly to her mom."

—NICOLAS, PARENT OF A THREE-YEAR-OLD

> *"It's discouraging to ask about gender equality measures and see the teachers get this blank look on their faces or hear them say: 'Sure, we have a plan, but we have to make time for the kids, too.'"*

—GEORGE, PARENT OF A THREE-YEAR-OLD

Parent: At my daughter's preschool, there's a room with dolls and a stove, and another room with LEGOs and cars. When I arrive, the girls are almost always in the doll room.

Many preschools create an environment with corners or rooms where they inadvertently separate traditional girls' and boys' toys. Ask the teachers what their thinking process is in designing the sections and placing the materials in the rooms. Ask them what measures they're taking to ensure that the children get to try a variety of games and develop a range of skills and roles.

For teachers: How do girls and boys use the toys and other materials and the spaces available at preschool? Talk to your colleagues and try to observe any patterns in how the children play. Have building materials in several spaces and see if that changes how they play. In the house area, include a broken mixer, telephone, and a tool box so that they can tinker and invent while they prepare food for the dolls. See about dividing spaces thematically rather than by the materials themselves. Create small worlds, like the aquarium room, the space room, and the garden room; this lets you combine materials and games in new ways. Create spaces and sort materials by colors: the red room, green room, or blue room. Find out more in the gender trap "Girl's Room, Boy's Room, Playroom" (page 44).

Parent: What can I do when the staff greet my daughter with a "Oh, what a pretty dress you're wearing today!"

Highlight other properties of the dress. Perhaps it has dots, stripes, colors, or something else that can be commented on. Or mention something else your child has done that morning or on the way to preschool. Try to shift the conversation to the child as a person, instead of continuing to talk about the child's appearance. Later, when the child isn't present, talk to the teachers and ask them about their thinking around focusing on children's appearances, like their clothes and their hair. Ask if there's a unified strategy among the staff for how they greet children. Explain that you think that it's important that your child is treated as a person, and that it shouldn't matter what they are wearing. Raise the clothing issue with other parents so that they can weigh in, too.

For teachers: Affirmation is a strong motivator for children. Some children will wear clothes to get recognition. What are your and your colleagues' ideas about clothing and looks for girls and boys, and how do those ideas influence how you interact with the children? What does it mean—to you—to treat children as individuals? See the gender trap "A Skull by Any Other Name . . ." (page 68) for more information.

Parent: What should I do when the teacher says it's natural for boys to fight and play with weapons?

Ask the teacher what they mean and what they're basing these ideas on. When something is seen as "natural" or "the way it is," it usually means that it's biological and thereby, supposedly, unchangeable. Biology can be used as a way of arguing against promoting gender equality. It could also be that the teacher is so locked into their conviction that they can only see situations that match their worldview. Like people who are pregnant and suddenly see baby carriages everywhere, teachers may notice boys who fight more than they notice boys who choose to do other things. This skewed perception is self-reinforcing.

For teachers: In private, people can have various opinions about gender-based differences. As a professional teacher, it's important to be able to rise above that. Discuss expectations and ideas about concepts like *girlish, boyish, manly,* and *womanly* with your colleagues. By laying bare your own values and ideas you can grow more aware of what you see and experience.

Challenge your thought patterns by looking for boys and girls who are doing something you think they don't usually do. Boys may very well be learning from each other to play weapons games with sticks. What children do and play is very much about what games are introduced, how those introductions play out, and what role models are available. Find out more in the gender trap "All She Does Is Cook, Anyway" (page 50).

Parent: It seems that all the songs they sing at preschool are about boys. How can I talk to the teachers about this?

If your child likes to sing, start by mentioning that you're so happy that they sing a lot at preschool. Then you can mention that you've noticed that almost all the songs seem to be about boys and ask if the teachers have noticed that, too. Often, something like that will be entirely unintentional and simply due to the fact that most songs, like most children's stories, are about boys, males, and men.

For teachers: Take a look at your collection of songs. What are the songs about? Add songs that describe boys and girls in more varied ways. Change songs around to make them more gender equal. Read more in the gender trap "Once Upon a Time" (page 38).

Parent: Sometimes when I come to pick up my child, the staff will tell me that the girls are inside and the boys are outside. I don't know how to respond.

Many people think it's natural for children to play in gender-segregated groups, and adults can have a hard time realizing that they are validating and reinforcing this. Try asking a question: *Oh, you had gender-segregated play groups today?* You can also ask what the pedagogical purpose behind the groups is. Part of the professional pedagogical task is to challenge children to try new games and to enter into relationships with different children. When we assume that girls have to be friends with girls and boys with boys, children miss out on a large number of friends.

For teachers: What happens when children are addressed as girls and boys, and what signals does that send to the children and to parents? Is it a coincidence that girls and boys are playing separately or is it a common occurrence? If they regularly play in gender-segregated groups, it's a good idea to create opportunities for children who don't regularly play together to try that. For more on this, see the gender trap "The Boys Are Over Here!" (page 126).

Parent: My child and two others took off all their clothes when they were playing, and the teachers were very upset. I didn't know what to say.

The teachers were probably upset because they were scared. Nudity is often associated with sexuality, and children's sexuality is still considered somewhat taboo. Talk about nudity and about how to convey to the children that their bodies are something positive, not something to feel shame or guilt about. Having an open attitude to the body contributes to healthy self-esteem.

For teachers: What is your approach to nude children? This subject is so loaded that it's often not discussed. But it's important for children to know that the body is something positive. As with other games, talk about how there are rules for bodies and for the genitals, the *snippa* and the *snopp*. It's important for children to learn that they are in control of their own bodies. Be clear with parents about your thinking on this and why. This will reassure them. For more on this, see the gender traps "What Do You Have Between Your Legs?" (page 212) and "Who Can Touch?" (page 214).

Gender equality is fun!

246

Parent: The preschool always calls me, the mom, when my child is sick, even though there's two of us as parents.

Moms often end up in the top slot in the contact list just out of habit, and often this is accompanied by the expectation that moms are primarily in charge of the kids. Explain to staff that you want to be treated equally as parents. Suggest that the preschool call you every other time if they're not able to call both of you.

For teachers: What do the school contact lists look like? Do preprinted forms list "mother's name" first? Forms can easily be changed to say *parent* rather than *mother* or *father*. That way, all family constellations can feel included. Contact all of a child's parents when something happens, not just the first one on the list or the one who lives the closest, unless the parents have expressly asked for that. It's also important for all parents to receive all the information that gets sent from the preschool, and to get to be part of what the children create in terms of drawings and other things. Treating parents gender-equally is part of promoting gender equality.

Parent: When we filled out the form for preschool, it said *Mother* and *Father*. It felt odd that our family wasn't included. We struck out the *Father* and wrote *Mother* and *Mother* instead. How should we address this with the school?

Some preschools think they only have children who live in traditional nuclear families and therefore don't have to have an approach that covers other family constellations, or that the issue isn't so important. The best thing to do is simply to explain that it's important for all families to feel included at preschool. Ask them to review their songs, books, and other materials to ensure that a variety of family constellations are included.

For teachers: If you work in an area with uniform family constellations, consider that it's important to prepare children for the rest of society and the diverse array of possible family constellations. This will help children show respect for differences instead of fearing them. Simply speaking of *parents*, instead of *mothers* and *fathers*, can improve matters a lot. It's important that the preschool reviews and changes forms, family trees, and stories so that all families can be represented. Remember that for children, their families are the most important thing to them, and all families are equal and should have equal space and visibility at preschool. Reading books that include various family constellations as a matter of fact is a good way to reflect the variety that exists in society. See the gender traps "Once Upon a Time" (page 38), "What's Your Dad's Name?" (page 120), and "Where Do You Live?" (page 117) for more on this.

Parent: The preschool says that they don't have time to work on both pedagogy and gender equality. How should I respond to that?

All teaching is built on values, whether conscious or subconscious. All teaching probably has some kind of gender perspective. Ask the teacher to clarify what they mean. Open questions are always good. Talk to the head of the preschool and explain that the teachers don't feel that they have time for gender equality measures.

For teachers: Try to avoid thinking of gender and gender equality as an extra project. Instead, see it as a way of thinking that accompanies all activities. In the beginning, it may take time to learn to think in new ways and to create a common knowledge base among the staff. Start by including gender equality as a fixed agenda item for weekly planning meetings, and plan and follow-up on the activities you start. Work on one small part at a time and start with the low-hanging fruit. Go through songs and books and other materials and determine how boys and girls, women and men, and nonbinary persons are portrayed and represented. Then, assess the language you use with children, how you acknowledge them, how they play, and so on. It's a good idea to bring in someone from outside, for instance, a colleague from another preschool, a gender pedagogue, or a gender equality consultant, because it's easy to be blind to these kinds of problems. Gender inequality thrives in everyday activities. Paradoxically, that's also where it's hardest to notice it. In time, a gender equality mindset will be as natural as your work on language development.

Parent: As a parent, how can I generate interest in gender issues and gender equality without being seen as tedious? I'm worried my child will suffer if the staff is annoyed with me.

Most teachers are professionals who can keep their opinions about parents separate from their work with children. Be honest, straightforward, and raise the issue even if it's hard. As a first step, talk to other parents; most likely, there are several who agree that gender equality is important. That way, you can raise the issue together. Try giving the teachers

curriculum-details
strategies for equal treatment
parent/teacher meeting

milk

a book on children and gender equality as a present. There are a number of books on this topic and most people are happy to receive a present. Organize a school meeting on gender and gender equality and suggest a speaker who can inspire and inform. Ask about the preschool's agenda for activities and their guidelines for the equal treatment of children, and ask that the staff present these at a meeting. Make an appointment to see the head of the preschool and explain that you think gender equality is important for your child and ask what the preschool's approach is for promoting gender equality.

For teachers: Consider a request from a parent an expression of interest in your work and an opportunity for improvement. Parents and preschools are in a codependent relationship that can be difficult for parents to handle. Many parents worry that their children will suffer the consequences if they themselves start asking uncomfortable questions. Demonstrate that you are a professional and can talk about your work. During the introductory period for new children, tell parents that you welcome their comments and questions about the preschool. Parents who are engaged with their children and with gender equality are an asset for both the children and the preschool.

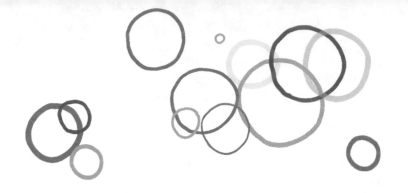

The Gender-Equal Preschool

In a gender-equal preschool, all children would be treated gender-equally and respectfully. The children would be given a diverse range of role models by the staff and through the materials the preschool uses. All children would learn methods for knowing where their own limits are, what feels good, and what does not. At a gender-equal preschool, children feel confident and know that all children are fantastic just the way they are. The school is a place for understanding and respecting each other. No one has to compromise their own integrity for fear of not being accepted or liked. The children would get to be the way they want to be and like whomever they want to like. Everyone would have the same worth and the concepts *normal* and *abnormal* wouldn't exist.

Practicing Gender Equality

Gender frames (noun) = Two sets of ideas about what's considered acceptable behavior for, and about what's expected of, girls/women and boys/men.

Open Your Eyes

We've been talking about gender traps and cruxes that create inequalities—inequalities in how children are treated and the opportunities they are afforded; when they play, how they are dressed, how their hair is styled; and how they are spoken to and about, are expected to speak; how and with whom they are expected to be friends, how they are expected to feel (and behave when they feel that way), and how they are supposed to feel about, use, and touch their own bodies. Bringing to light these inequalities and their consequences is a first step toward improving gender equality. We've also offered suggestions for how adults can fairly simply offer children more opportunities in everyday situations. These suggestions focus on how we can help our children challenge and go beyond the narrow gender frames society imposes on them. Like gender traps, gender frames are insidious, restricting choices and controlling behavior in all areas of life, everything from clothes, to body language, to career aspirations, to romantic partners. Girls and women are expected to be and behave as prescribed by the "feminine" frame, and boys and men are expected to be and behave as prescribed by the "masculine" frame. And nonbinary people are often presumed not to exist, at all. These frames are often invisible and implicit—they're taken for granted—making them hard to change.

Within the Frame

Generally speaking, we're not aware of these gender frames until someone colors outside of them. At that point, we'll often quickly respond to "police" them and direct them back inside the frame. The policing can be subtle or blatant. A boy wearing a dress can be made invisible, erased, disregarded, ignored. Or scolded: *Boys don't wear dresses!*; mocked: *Halloween was last month!*; or threatened: *I'm gonna hurt you, you little . . . !*

Parents, other adults, siblings, friends, and books and films are responsible for policing behavior that challenges gender frames. Very young children can be quite quick to correct other children and adults who venture outside the frame. Children learn that they will be praised—they'll receive positive affirmation from the people around them—when they stay within the prescribed frames. Staying within a given gender frame can feel safe, because the frame provides us with a ready-made set of rules for what to do and how to

255

be. The policing and the praising serve to transmit gender frames from one generation to the next and make them part of what we call our culture. If we want to promote gender equality, we need to pay attention to when we police and correct children and when they police and correct each other, and why.

What Has Value?

Gender frames come with expectations about characteristics and behavior, but also with attributions of value. Characteristics and behaviors traditionally considered "masculine" have long been considered more valuable than those that are labeled "feminine." In most cases, girls and women who approach the masculine are perceived as advancing to the next level. Boys and men who transgress against the male gender frame are not afforded the same latitude. Instead, they'll be told that they're weak. The idea that the traditionally masculine is more valuable than the traditionally feminine is firmly entrenched in our culture. Creating gender equality is in part about questioning and changing this power imbalance in private and public life.

Complementing Each Other

Gender frames include ideas about who is supposed to fall in love with whom. Many people take for granted that girls should fall in love with boys and vice versa; heterosexuality is made normative. Homophobia becomes a way of policing people whose choice of partners challenges gender frames. The idea that everyone is heterosexual is based on the notion that women and men are opposites and that masculinity and femininity complement each other to form a whole. This way of thinking will often reduce gender equality to a number. Once there are an equal number of men and women in a committee or on a board—presto—gender equality has supposedly been achieved. But numbers don't necessarily speak to content. A group with an equal number of men and women may still be one in which only the men are really heard. That's not gender equality. Similarly, when men who, for instance, work at a preschool, are assigned all the tasks traditionally labeled "male," like playing ball or doing carpentry, that's not gender equality. In order to promote gender equality, we have to challenge the idea that men and women are each other's opposites that complement each other and realize that individuals can complement each other irrespective of their genders.

What Kind of Society Do We Want?

Some people claim that gender frames are based on biological differences between women and men. But if that were the case, why all the policing? Why is so much time spent teaching children to be girls and boys? And why do the ways in which the labels "girlish" and "boyish" are applied change over time? There are, of course, differences among people: we're different heights, have different color hair, and so on. Some people are cautious, extroverted, happy, sad, responsible, reckless, angry, or kind. But these characteristics don't readily sort into *girlish* and *boyish*, *womanly* and *manly*.

Some people point to history and claim that men and women have always been different. But history is always interpreted based on the interpreter's own experiences and their culture. For example, previous generations of researchers missed the fact that women used to hunt. The weapons in women's graves were interpreted as gifts. When we try to understand other animals and their lives, our own filters become obvious. Most animals have been described as heterosexual—a proposition that's being called into question by more and more research. Both nature and history allow for a lot more variation than we might have thought. Furthermore, irrespective of what we think is biologically determined, there's no reason to let biological differences justify discriminating against girls, boys, women, nonbinary people, or men. Suppose someone is forgetful and this characteristic is genetically determined. Legally speaking, they still need to pay their bills when they're due. Similarly, we can't explain to the police that we have a natural urge to speed and expect not to get a ticket.

Not all boys are tough. Some are small and thin, and others are large and round. Not all girls are pretty and nice. Some are temperamental and take up a lot of space. Others are cautious. Despite this obvious variation, many people stubbornly insist on referring to those outside traditional norms as anomalies. Children are told that they are tomboys or "a little different." As adults, they're called unwomanly, unmanly, mannish, or effeminate. If we were to validate diversity and stop trying to doggedly force people into rigid gender frames, we would probably be able to see that the variation among girls or among boys is just as great as that between girls and boys.

Different Strategies, Same Goal

"When I read Winnie-the-Pooh, *I usually let Tigger and Owl be girl animals, since there are hardly any girls in that story."*

—MOSES, PARENT OF A THREE-YEAR-OLD

"My daughter has a pink gymnastics uniform with a tutu. I tell her she can jump higher than anyone and is super cool in her pink suit."

—ÅSA, PARENT OF A FIVE-YEAR-OLD

"I don't want my daughter to be seen as a cute princess. I don't think girls need any more of that. What they do need is to develop their self-esteem and understand that they're important. People tilting their heads at them and telling them they're adorable isn't part of that."

—KLARA, PARENT OF A FOUR-YEAR-OLD

The suggestions in this book have included three kinds of strategies for improving gender equality: redistributing, reconceiving, and rejecting. *Redistributing* is a quantitative strategy that can be used when the numbers are very imbalanced in terms of girls and boys. Redistributing is a first step toward gender equality and can involve changing songs and stories so that the protagonists include girls, nonbinary children, and boys by replacing some of the he/him roles. *Reconceiving* seeks to give new meaning and values to clothes, toys, and feelings, in order to expand our conceptions of what children can be and do and unskew the power dynamics between masculinity and femininity. *Rejecting* means setting aside toys, clothes, books, and other things that reinforce gender frames, because not everything can be reconceived. Adults may feel that children are better off without gender-stereotyped items and attributes. The three strategies can be combined. Which ones we choose will depend on how we think about gender equality and the kind of environment a child is growing up in. Giving new meaning to colors and other things can be a lot easier if the environment is somewhat open and gender equal, because children won't be as strictly prodded into gender frames in those situations.

Letting children adopt and adapt to a gender frame can seem like a simple short-term solution; they'll probably receive positive affirmation from the adults and children around them. The tricky part of gender traps is that changing them requires taking action. Often, it's simply easier to stay trapped and let the gender frames rule. But when children are forced into a rigid frame, they cannot develop fully as unique individuals. Supporting them and their ideas may feel hard at first, but, for the children, it'll be worth the effort in terms of their confidence and self-esteem.

Reactions to the three strategies typically vary. Rejecting is generally taken as more of an expression of a political ideology than the two other strategies. But isn't giving children gender-stereotyped toys and clothes as ideological as it is to reject those items? Rejecting sugar or additives that aren't good for our children's bodies is not at all as controversial as rejecting gender stereotypes. The important thing with all three strategies is to see that the same ambition underpins each one: to create more opportunities for all children and a more gender-equal society.

When Worlds Collide

"Come on, Dad, let's play hotel! You be the guest, and I'll clean. Filip can be the manager."
"Don't you think you ought to be the manager? Filip is only two."

"No, I can't be the manager."
"Why not?"
"Dad, I'm a girl. Girls can't be managers."

Sometimes, our desire to offer children equal opportunities clashes with the reality they see and experience. In general, the world they face is not gender equal. More men than women are bosses; more firefighters are men, while more nurses are women. We can choose to insist that girls can be managers and boys can be nurses, but the incongruity between what children see and what we say can make it hard for them to understand us.

If we instead start from their experience of the world, affirming it, we can help them understand what we are saying. Yes, more men are bosses, but women can also be bosses. To make clear that things can change, we can say, *Yes, people used to believe that only men could be bosses, but now we know that's not right.* We can talk about parenting in the same way: *In the old days, daddies weren't allowed to stay home with their children because almost everyone thought that mommies were better at taking care of children. But now we know that both mommies and daddies can take care of children.* The older the child, the more we can talk with them about what gender equality is and about how things can change and aren't set in stone. Challenging ideas about what's girlish and boyish, and giving children the strength to find their own paths, becomes easier and easier.

Children Do as We Do

"We think gender equality is very important in raising our two kids. Julius and Minna both help their dad whenever he's fixing his car, and they both help me with the cooking."

—ANNIKA, PARENT OF A FOUR-YEAR-OLD AND SIX-YEAR-OLD

Change can be scary. We prefer the known to the unknown, so we resist change. By continuing along in our old ways, we don't have to handle the uncertainty that comes with change. We let whoever is better at baking brownies bake the brownies, and the one who's better at mowing the lawn mows the lawn. The alternative is for us to challenge ourselves and try new things. Gender equality requires role models. If we as adults don't increase our repertoires, we won't come across as credible to our children when we talk about and try to promote gender equality. Being able to change things—stepping outside gender frames and trying new things—is only possible if we feel safe and secure. This sense of security can be generated when we validate each other—when we let each other know that we're fine just the way we are. Positive affirmation helps create an atmosphere where there's plenty of room for daring to try, where failing is an accepted part of the process. This makes it easier and more fun to try new things and to make change. With a gender-equal approach to both adults and children, we can erase the two gender frames and create more opportunities, more ways of being. We no longer need to police ourselves and others for fear of not fitting in. We have more fun, more fairness, and more adventures this way, when we parent and play.

Advice on the Road to Gender Equality

Take the initiative and make sure things turn out the way you wish they would. Start from a basis of assuming that everyone thinks gender equality is a good thing.

Don't apologize. You don't always have to explain why you do things a certain way. Try to be as casual in going beyond gender frames as others are in staying within them.

If something's a good thing, validate it, and build on that, even if it's small and seems inconsequential. Positive affirmations matter.

Constructive suggestions are good. Offer alternatives rather than only highlighting problems.

Accept that some will consider you weird and tedious. Essentially everyone who challenges things that others take for granted will experience this kind of response at times.

Feeling like you're alone in this can be hard. Find support from others who share your perspective.

Ask other parents, relatives, and teachers to explain their behavior and reasoning. This lets them share their thoughts, and you don't have to be the one who has to justify your approach all the time.

Respect the fact that not everyone will share your view or want to act on it the way you do. There's room for a range of views.

Be prepared for people to be defensive. Do not take it personally.

By creating gender equality in your everyday life, you are doing a lot. You only have a direct influence on what you yourself do; serving as a role model for others goes a long way.

Talk. Discuss. Highlight gender-equal role models and exciting topics debated in the media.

Choose not to participate in activities and events that you don't think are positive for you or your children.

Challenging norms takes energy. Pick your battles. Some days, you might have to just go with the flow. Don't be too hard on yourself.

Checking In

Every now and then, someone will wonder whether gender equality has gone too far. We, the authors, find this odd. Do people who worry about gender equality going too far also worry about people being too healthy? It's frightening to realize that advocates for extending suffrage to women probably were asked the same kind of question, at the beginning of the last century. Today, we're certainly glad they didn't pay any attention to those voices of "moderation." As advocates of gender equality, we're also told that we're impatient, and that we ought to think of how much things have already changed and be happy with that. Naturally we're happy. But that doesn't mean that we can a turn a blind eye to the fact that our children's opportunities are still tied to their biological sex. Just because something has improved doesn't mean it's good. We can clearly see that gender inequality affects our children if we consider how gender traps and cruxes show up in all aspects of their lives, molding them.

My grandmother was 56 when she could vote for the first time.

Looking back at history, it's obvious that ideas about what girls and boys, women and men, can and should be and do are not immutable. We can also see that we, the people, have the power to change and shape the world we want our children to grow up in. This is clear when it comes to the environment and ecology. The greater the demand for organic food and environmentally friendly transportation, the greater the supply, and the more common these become in everyday life. Items labeled fair trade, organic, certified humane, and so on show up to meet that growing demand.

My grandfather had to go to jail when he didn't want to do military service.

The more we demand, and the more of us that demand, that our children be treated as individuals, not as girls or boys, the more other parents, teachers, doctors, caregivers, and other important people in our children's lives will pay attention to how they treat them. Conceiving of gender equality as a kind of quality is still in its early stages. Some preschools have a gender-equal profile, some publishers gender

My dad stayed home with me when I was little, but he didn't get any time off when my older siblings were born.

check their books, and some clothing stores are focusing on gender-neutral clothes marketed to all children. But there's a lot of work left to do, and we hope this is just the beginning of an exciting gender equality journey. We also hope that our book will inspire a fun conversation on how we can create a more gender-equal world for our children. If we take small steps and make changes in our everyday existence, we can make a big difference, together. Hopefully, our children and grandchildren will have reason to thank us in much the same way that we thank the previous generation's advocates for gender equality.

Acknowledgments

THANK YOU . . .

. . . to Martin, Inez, Emelie, Hedvig, and Clara for being in our lives and for constantly challenging us.

And thanks also to everyone who has supported us and cheered us on in our writing and thinking.

A special thank you to Ana Larsson for being a fantastic sounding board and having an awesome eye for structure, and to researcher Klara Dolk for her upside-down-turning expertise.

Thanks also to Martin Henkel, Tina Tomičić, Erik Ebbeson, and Herbert Henkel for encouraging us when we took our first faltering steps, and to Ina Petterson, Margareta Henkel, and Daniel Andersson for your careful reading and exclamation points as we approached the end.

Thank you everyone who has contributed stories and voices from the real world. Without you, this book would never have existed.

Thanks to all the survey respondents at FOFF (Forum for Feminist Parents).

Thanks to the heads of information at Lindex, design at Polarn O. Pyret, children's clothing at KappAhl, communications at BRIO, and sales at BR Toys/TOP-TOY, along with communications directors at the preschools in Norrköping, Spånga-Tensta, and Hägersten-Liljeholmen who responded to our questions about children and gender equality.

About the Authors

Kristina Henkel is a gender equality consultant in pre-K–12. She runs the educational organization Jämställt.se and is the author of *En jämställd förskola* (A Gender-Equal Preschool). Kristina is the parent of one small and one medium child.

Marie Tomičić is a researcher and teacher, teaching leadership and creativity. She operates the publishing company OLIKA which promotes diversity in children's literature. Marie is the parent of one large and two small children.

Mia Lidbom is a graphic designer. She designs books, information, product packaging, brochures, and advertising distinguished by thought and function. In 2002, Mia received the *Utmärkt Svensk Form* (Exemplary Swedish Design) award.

Emili Svensson is an illustrator of magazines and books, often focused on children. Her illustrations convey feelings with a lot of humor. You can find her images in *Normkreativitet i förskolan* (Creative Norms in Preschool) and *Ta makten* (Claim Power).